GIRLS' LITERACY EXPERIENCES IN AND OUT OF SCHOOL

How do American girls compose and amend their identities? In this text, prominent scholars in their respective fields examine the complex social and cultural constructions that shape girls' lives both in and out of school. The book looks at matters ranging from embedded issues of class, race, ethnicity, immigrant status, and sexuality to popular culture and personal histories.

Exploring the scholarly literature on gender and education, the successes and failures of feminist pedagogy, and girls' practices with both traditional and non-traditional texts, as well as the primary sources of a material culture, the authors expose the myriad forces that script girls' gender, identity, and literacy. The distinctive contribution of this book is to open up new discussions of girls in American classrooms today and to critically examine their experiences as they navigate preconceived notions of who they are while forming their personal and public identities.

Elaine J. O'Quinn is Professor, English Department, Appalachian State University, USA.

GIRLS' LITERACY EXPERIENCES IN AND OUT OF SCHOOL

Learning and Composing Gendered Identities

Edited by Elaine J. O'Quinn

Routledge
Taylor & Francis Group

NEW YORK AND LONDON

First published 2013
by Routledge
711 Third Avenue, New York, NY 10017

Simultaneously published in the UK
by Routledge
2 Park Square, Milton Park, Abingdon, Oxon OX14 4RN

Routledge is an imprint of the Taylor & Francis Group, an informa business

Library of Congress Cataloging in Publication Data
Girls' literacy experiences in and out of school : learning and composing
gendered identities / edited by Elaine O'Quinn.
p. cm.
Includes bibliographical references and index.
1. Teenage girls--Education--United States. 2. Literacy--Social aspects--
United States. 3. Teenage girls--Books and reading--United States. 4. Young
adult literature. 5. Teenage girls--United States--Social conditions.
6. Women--United States--Identity. I. O'Quinn, Elaine.
LC1755.G57 2012
373.182352--dc23
2011052863

ISBN: 978-0-415-89736-5 (hbk)
ISBN: 978-0-415-89737-2 (pbk)
ISBN: 978-0-203-80213-7 (ebk)

Typeset in Bembo
by Taylor & Francis Books

Printed and bound in the United States of America by
Walsworth Publishing Company, Marceline, MO.

For Mom
We were always girls together.

CONTENTS

FOREWORD

Rachel Simmons

My girlhood snapshot: Loud. Competitive. Big. Hilarious. Opinionated. Peers always included me, yet I was unbearably different. Growing up in a small religious school didn't help. Inside, I rankled with fear that something might be wrong with me; English class was forty-three minutes of the possibility that there wasn't. In the hallways at school I felt quietly alone and invisible, but like Narnia perched at the back of the closet, English class revealed a new hallway teeming with characters that looked and sounded like me, and—better yet—represented the "me" I might become.

As an educator and author who studies girls' development, I am proud to introduce this remarkable volume of essays about girls and their particular place in English Language Arts classrooms. It is long overdue. Growing up girl today is a tangle of contradictions. At a moment when girls have more opportunities than ever, they face pressure from the culture to embrace versions of themselves that compromise their potential and emerging sense of who they will be. They see the sexy girl, taught to use her body as a tool of power. They note the aggressive girl, who uses force to access confidence. They are taught to be the "good" girl, desperate to be perfect and please others at any cost. But nowhere do they see the girl they know is evolving inside. This text offers a glimpse of girls as they are, considers the things they are concerned with, and provides an opportunity to think about how to build on what they desire and make it work to their advantage.

The English classroom can blunt the limiting personas of the public face of girls by providing possibilities for their unique selves: selves who can embrace being different, who know they are understood, who are not afraid of being seen, who are willing to take risks and try new things. Strong female literary characters, expressions of social consciousness, and a self acquired through reflective composition are a counterpoint to culture's suffocating grip on girl identity, and we can do much to show girls capabilities they may never have imagined for themselves through these venues. I was no exception to the rescue of reading and writing.

In elementary school, I built my own ragtag posse of outspoken girls from books like *Harriet the Spy*, *A Wrinkle in Time*, and *Starring Sally J. Freedman as Herself*, and it was in my senior English class that I finally disclosed I was gay. I did it by writing creatively in the voice of another character, a character I could bring to life in ways that were important to me. Both of these outlets were a crucial stop on the road not only to coming out but to believing in myself and understanding that who I was and what I thought mattered. At school, it was only in English class that I was allowed the space to explore this.

Today, girls have the good fortune of knowing an even wider range of characters that can guide them through the teen years and beyond by validating what they know to be true about themselves and the world they live in. They have a variety of ways to voice their opinions and consider their options. If the societal "rules" of being a girl make honest self-expression risky, even punishable, English class has the potential to invert those constraints, providing girls with a multitude of channels to express emotions and thoughts and ideas that might otherwise stay tucked away.

For girls raised to be nice at all costs, English is a porous access point for authenticity. Female characters that speak their minds and make a difference (despite *their* differences) give readers permission to do the same. Narratives of the self and others provide cover for girls to try on new desires and dreams and to work through personal challenges. Secrets and truths are safely inscribed onto pages only a trusted teacher may see or brought to discussion in a community groomed to be accepting and open to all. These acts of sharing and being affirmed are the raw material of agency. They give girls the sense that they have the power to make a contribution to the world and that they are a person worthy of being heard.

English classrooms offer avenues of escape for girls. For those who are suffering, literature and composition may become a refuge, a place to leave behind the anguish of an imploding friendship or a messy parental divorce or, just as importantly, a place to write about or create around those issues without fear. For girls burdened by privilege, egocentrism, prejudices, or social alienation, the English classroom can open doors to understanding new cultures as well as expanded ideas about identity. Girls sometimes find it hard to move beyond the moment and the belief that life is always as it appears; but as they grapple intimately with the decisions of their favorite characters, assess increased knowledge of the world they inhabit, and participate in virtual relationships that activate empathy and global consciousness, inspire perspective, encourage action, and provide a chance for social change, they refine the internal machinery necessary to face their own choices and judgments, learning even that they can safely and purposefully act on those realizations.

Whether it's through social media and the Internet, young adult novels, meaningful learning tasks, open discussions, or some form of personal writing, girls have always used multiple forms of literacy to determine who they are. The very essence of English class wants to know: What do you think? How do you feel? Why? This book explores the multitude of ways girls may answer these questions, including—and especially—ways we may never have intended.

ACKNOWLEDGMENTS

I owe a big thank you to many people for helping me complete this book, but I would like especially to thank the following: Naomi Silverman, editor par excellence, who believed so much in this project and responded always with gracious kindness to help me over each hurdle I encountered; all the people at Routledge who work behind the scenes every day to make those of us out front look good; all the contributors who were so purposeful and insightful in their writing; Rachel Simmons for taking the time from a very busy schedule to write the foreword because she cares in all ways about the trials girls face; my friends David and Colin who supported me with humor and weekly decompressing outings so that I could work with a clear mind the rest of the week; my niece Ausha who, from the moment I first mentioned the project, kept after me with "are you finished yet?"; the reviewers who took their time for my project; all the girls out there who remind me daily of the work still left to be done on their behalf. And an extra-special "I could not have done it without you" shout-out to Jim, Izzy, and Ashton who give new meaning to the word loving; you three rock.

Elaine J. O'Quinn

INTRODUCTION

Elaine J. O'Quinn

In *The Dialectic of Freedom* (1988) Maxine Greene discusses the importance of naming the obstacles that stand in the way of enhanced possibilities. She makes pointed connections between education, private lives, and freedom, insisting that we remain vigilant about how "reality" is constituted and attuned to the socially imposed barriers that keep many from forming a more authentic self. "When people cannot name alternatives, imagine a better state of things, share with others a project of change," says Greene," they are likely to remain anchored or submerged, even as they proudly assert their autonomy" (9). I think of Maxine Greene's words whenever gender becomes a part of my classroom discussion. Until they reflect upon what lies behind their unreflective beliefs about gender and the part it plays in decisions that influence schools, literacy politics, and their own emerging identities, students initially deem they have no serious concerns. However, once we begin to break apart what it means for schools to serve a student's particular interests, needs, and desires rather than the school's own demands for bureaucratic efficiency, dispassionate authority, and cultural tradition, such arguments begin to thin. Students start to recognize that they are tethered to a system that mostly allows only limited freedom, false choices, and little space for personal agency and growth. They begin to realize that they have assumed the conditions and roles of their education as something fixed and final rather than something still open, possible, and hence alterable. Because literacy is viewed in schools as something that is fairly predictable and measurable, students do not consider that what constitutes their developing young adult literacy may be quite different from the literacies they were encouraged to embrace as children. It is at this point we can begin to talk about the authenticity of their school lives.

This Project

A number of years have passed since an initial wave of literacy researchers presented informative and sometimes alarming and controversial reports of how girls perform their lives in and out of school. From broad based accounts such as Myra and David Sadker's *Failing at Fairness* (1994) and the AAUW's *How Schools Shortchange Girls* (1992) through the close studies of Mary Pipher's *Reviving Ophelia* (1994), Peggy Orenstein's *Schoolgirls* (1995), and Margaret Finder's *Just Girls* (1997), scholars have continually expanded how they investigate and write about the psychological, sociological, educational, and anthropological lives of girls, though the focus on girls' literacy needs has diminished. Further, very little attention has been paid to the changing literacy needs of girls as they move from childhood into their teen years. This text aims to open up that conversation.

In recent years, an academic field known as Girls' Studies has emerged that expands on all of the aforementioned disciplines to include politics, history, religion, sexuality, and popular as well as material culture. A growing number of universities, such as my own, now offer minors and/or certificates in Girls' Studies. The field should not be thought of as synonymous with the now consumerized Girl Power movement, attributed in part to pop groups like the Spice Girls, but as rooted in the political reclamation of the word "girl" by activists like the Riot Grrrls and in an early African-American hip-hop culture intended to encourage strong black females (Gonick 2008). While the popular discourses of girlhood are a presence in Girls' Studies, the field itself has interdisciplinary scholarly appeal. It moves beyond the public schoolhouse gate and any one classroom subject, bringing with it interests and concerns that in the past may not have been properly considered when looking at traditions of something as specific as literacy education. The intent of this volume of essays is to bring much of what we have learned about girls through Girls' Studies to the English classroom. By including issues ordinarily left outside school into language arts conversations about girls' literacy experiences and gendered identities as they become more mature readers, writers and creators of text, the chapter authors blur the lines between the private and public personas of girls and challenge the idea that the two should or can be separated.

There are also personal reasons for this project. As a teacher, I still remember Connie, who came to my desk crying at the end of a class because I had assigned a pre-reading collage for *Romeo and Juliet* that was to represent student feelings about romantic love. "I'm gay," she tearfully told me. "I can't make a collage that is honest about who I am. You won't be able to hang it in the room, and I won't be able to explain it to the class." I think of Mai La eating lunch day after day in my classroom because she was too shy to eat in the lunchroom among those she considered strangers, quietly telling me her culture made her feel so different from her classmates. I consider my own niece, the best reader in her class for many years and winner of numerous school writing awards, who, during her teen years, was suddenly loath to pick up a book or write even a paragraph, preferring most times to do her reading online and her writing through social media boards and text messaging. Stories of uncertainty and not being accepted or recognized in personally important ways abound in the lives of girls. This project was conceived in order that we might further consider literacy practices that can help validate girls not only in their gendered identities, but also in their understanding of place, culture, and personal expression.

What the reader will find in this text is how the English classroom can applaud, confirm, explore, and engage the thoughts and actions of girls. The authors take a close look at teaching experiences, their interests in and concerns for the well-being of girls, and their understandings of how literacy and identity are linked together. With those key perceptions in mind, they begin to fill in the surrounding conversational gaps. They provide a number of missing pieces to the girlhood puzzle, trying not to improve girls but to enable them. They examine not only what is often implied about girls and literacy, but also what is hidden and what is unquestionably assumed. The girls they reference do more than read, write, and engage in projects. When encouraged, they go a step further. Given the proper tools, we learn that girls can embrace their literacy and find meaningful ways to connect the personal with the public. Through thoughtful consideration of the texts that surround them, the girls included in many of these chapters show that it is possible to transcend the restrained dimensions of conventional school experiences and expectations. By suggesting it is curriculum more so than girls that should be made accommodating, these authors encourage a contemporary re-examination of schools and their language arts classrooms and the ongoing sites of gender identity resistance found therein. Such exploration continues to be of critical importance to those invested in feminist educational studies and the unraveling of hegemonic discourses.

The Chapters

Social, cultural, technological, and political spheres of consideration are opened up to various degrees by all of the contributing authors. By providing positive, diverse scripts, the authors ask readers to begin thinking differently about the existing scripts concerning girls and their literacy needs both in and out of school and how those scripts may not be sufficient in allowing girls to present and grow their more genuine selves. In short, they give us some unique glimpses into the lives of some girls and invite us to build on what they offer. Similarly, the authors assemble their theoretical, methodological, and textual approaches differently, thereby showing us that there is no single, all embracing interpretation of girls, nor should there be. The needs, issues, and concerns of girls will only yield to a multi-perspective approach to which you, the reader, are urged to contribute as you read. The chapters are sectioned into parts to provide a way of moving through, thinking about, and making connections in the text; however, they can be read separately and in any order. The common thread that runs through all of the chapters is an urging to know and support girls in who they are and all they are yet to be. To that end, the contributors offer up a variety of complex viewpoints and considerations.

In Chapter 1, Jane Greer establishes a critical framework for the literacy projects taken on by the other authors. She provides a succinct and lively history of how girls have always used their schooling to either employ or transgress the rules of literacy imposed upon them. Greer shows girls in various settings doing what they must do in order to get what they need through reading and writing, and, in contemporary terms, other media sources. She challenges readers to ask how the structures and assumptions of education often ignore and misinterpret girls and their capabilities and notes with examples how girls have always subverted their officially acquired school literacies for their own ends. The ensuing authors take up Greer's summons in an array of meaningful and insightful considerations that show girls continuing to struggle with their evolving sense of self through a number of literacy venues.

Building on the strength and resilience of girls as documented by Greer, Linda Rice next considers how looking at Young Adult Historical Fiction with female protagonists through the lens of four major themes of challenge and perseverance can allow modern girls a vivid glimpse into the complexity of their own lives. Through a wide range of sample classroom activities that make the unfamiliar familiar, Rice helps students make sense in new ways of the many hardships girls encounter both at home and in the world. She, like Mary Napoli in Chapter 5, notes how through reading and focused response girls are able to add a dimension of reflective social consciousnesses to their own personhood. Rice invites girls into activities that allow them to see that emotional strength and courage is built, not assumed, and carries with it a challenge to grow in ways perhaps not previously considered.

For Rosemary Horowitz and Joanne Brown writing in Chapter 3, identity is not found simply in location. Together they take the bound places of immigration and through the metaphor of journey open up new lines of movement and new avenues of freedom. From girlhood to womanhood, a line is drawn that depicts this difficult crossing as a time of growth and discovery leading to personal and social empowerment, similar in some ways to the immigration experience itself. Though they recognize that the positioning of geography shapes individuals, the authors also contend that the psychological trajectories of journey deepen important understandings of self and the world. While reminding us of the incredible struggles of immigrant girls to find their place, Horowitz and Brown also show us the strength of character they are able to pull from within as they navigate what they know of old worlds while discovering so much about the new.

Perhaps no girl is more invisible or more threatened by visibility than the one who identifies as LGBTQ. In all the discussion that currently surrounds diversity, the dominant culture expectation about girls, sexuality, and femininity is still rarely discussed but always assumed. To help students become more accepting of a wider range of sexualities, Beth Younger, in Chapter 4, bravely suggests that educators need to be more forthcoming with students about the possibilities of what constitutes femininity and what that means or does not mean. She encourages readers to consider how we validate girls who may or may not be culturally approved in their degree of femininity, using a select set of texts to show us a spectrum of possibility. Literature should and can provide for the ways girls exist in the world, and Younger suggests that readers consider how the English classroom might support LGBTQ girls who are generally erased in the literature available in school.

Exposing girls to the larger world in order that they might see something of their immediate one is an idea explored by Mary Napoli through a summer reading club she conducted with six teenage girls. By exploring how global texts and culture impact local understandings of repression and inequities, the girls in Napoli's study begin to render the strange more familiar. As they uncover the social injustices experienced by girls worldwide, the girls in the club recognize the need to stand up for issues of social biases closer to home. Napoli's study clearly shows that with adult guidance girls can learn much about themselves by looking closely at girls with vastly different experiences.

Dawn Kirby engages girls with nonfiction in order to help them think and write about their lives as a means of self-discovery. Through Contemporary Memoir, she shows how girls are constantly developing their literacy practices and values, arriving at not only improved writing, but also deepened awareness of self and others. Kirby is able to help the girls of her study think about and respond to the recursive nature of text through modeling and exploring a range of literacy activities. She watches them move from the act of creating fan fiction to that of examining and writing about more personal experiences, showing them along the way that what they question and reflect on in their own lives is a way to facilitate growth.

In Chapter 7, Katie Kapurch argues that schools do not give girls enough credit for the autonomous literacies they consistently perform in relation to popular culture. Specifically, she cites the *Twilight* Saga, maintaining that girls gain agency in their spin-off creations of the kinds of texts that many adults believe steal agency. Kapurch troubles the literacy implications of pop culture by suggesting that girls' connection to it is more complex than may appear. She asserts that girls have active, not passive, responses to popular culture texts and media and that when they appropriate technology in ways of their own choosing, their literacy is increased. Girls are never the sum of any one kind of text, and Kapurch gives us compelling examples that show why.

Shayla Thiel-Stern applauds the successes of girls engaged in online citizen journalism production, while recognizing the limits of the feminist classroom, even when the teacher consistently engages in feminist practices. She discovers that attitudes and situations beyond the teacher's control play a major role in how successful a literacy experience can be, no matter how emancipating or open. For Shayla, connecting the ways girls are represented in media by teaching them to use the tools of media practitioners for their own ends allows them to (re)present themselves in the more meaningful way of investigation and analysis and encourages more transformative awareness. Her work offers some surprising results about our assumptions concerning girls and media.

Coming full circle, Karen Coats and Roberta Seelinger Trites ask readers once again to consider what we know historically about issues of gender, identity, and pedagogy, though through a different lens than Greer offers. They begin by examining a brief historical trajectory of critical thinking and its links to feminism and secondary English education. They then explore with classroom teachers the hurdles encountered as they offer students the opportunity to critically consider gender in the English classroom. The problems confronted are somewhat different from those the teachers of Thiel-Stern's study were faced with, but they help to further show the resistances that those who believe in feminist pedagogies may need to plan for and expect. To put into context what they learned in their research, the authors use two Young Adult novels to strengthen their premise that gender is a multivariate social construct, concluding that YA novels may provide a way to break down the stereotypes of gender so deeply ingrained in our social consciousness.

What Next?

What becomes clear in each chapter that follows is that girls and their literacy choices and habits are ever evolving. Their practices are positioned not only by gender, but also by numerous other social markers. Whether they are making music videos, engaging in online social media, writing themselves into fan fiction, or subverting institutional missions in order to attain personal visions of their own lives, girls cannot simply be erased or dismissed when they do not conform to our traditional expectations. These authors demonstrate that if we truly intend to know girls in all of their cultural struggles and practices, we must begin to integrate what they are telling us about themselves into the work we do with them both in and out of school. We need, as Finders suggested almost fifteen years ago, a pedagogy that considers and then acts on the ways we continue to silence and alienate certain girls. On the surface, the notions of girls and girlhood may appear not to have changed very much over time, especially when we look at the many adult produced understandings of them. However, when we take the time to actually talk to girls and consider the many paths they walk, we realize that there is a quiet revolution going on among them, and they will conduct it with or without our help. The authors of these chapters open up many arenas of consideration, and they all do it with a similar objective in mind: making the lives of girls better, more understandable, worthy, and worthy of study. Because girls continue to get so little formal attention, much work is still to be done on their behalf. We have barely scratched the surface of what it means to be a girl in our times. It is my hope that this text will inspire new and seasoned teachers, scholars, and advocates to move the conversation forward and in the process help all of us understand anew what it means to be a girl in every sense of the word.

Works Cited

American Association of University Women's Education Foundation and Wellesley College Center for Research on Women. *How Schools Shortchange Girls*. Washington, DC: American Association of University Women's Education Foundation, 1992. Print.

Finders, Margaret. *Just Girls: Hidden Literacies and Life in Junior High*. New York: Teachers College Press, 1997. Print.

Gonick, Marnina. "Girl Power." *Girl Culture: An Encyclopedia*. Eds. Claudia A. Mitchell and Jacqueline Reid-Walsh. Westport, CT: Greenwood Press, 2008. 310–14. Print.

Greene, Maxine. *The Dialectic of Freedom*. New York: Teachers College Press, 1988. Print.

Orenstein, Peggy. *Schoolgirls: Young Women, Self-Esteem, and the Confidence Gap*. New York: Doubleday, 1995. Print.

Pipher, Mary. *Reviving Ophelia*. New York: G.P. Putnam's Sons, 1994. Print.

Sadker, Myra and Sadker, David. *Failing at Fairness: How America's Schools Cheat Girls*. New York: Simon and Schuster, 1994. Print.

PART I

Girls and Literacy

A Historical Overview

1

"THE ORDER OF THE SCROLL"

Surveying Girls' Literacy Performances in and out of School, 1885–2011

Jane Greer

In the first weeks of 1912, Dorothy Allen Brown, a student at Manual Training High School in Kansas City, Missouri, penned in her diary:

> I intend to establish a secret society. This one is something new and extremely secret. No one, in fact, knows anything about it but me. ... Even the other members are not to know of their membership, especially as some are dead. ... I shall call it The Order of the Scroll because it is through books and reading that we know each other. I want one member from each century, at least one. She may have any country or station. She may be a queen or a scrubwoman. The character may be real or fictitious. The only requirement is that she be one who has done some one thing that "helped."

In subsequent entries, Dorothy acknowledges that she only "has the tail feathers of ... [an] idea," and considers Joan of Arc, Rebecca of Sunnybrook Farm, Maid Marian, Lady Jane Grey, Queen Victoria, and others as possible members for her society. Her "Order of the Scroll" is intriguing for what it tells us about her literacies—Brown is writing characters encountered in her reading, historical and fictional, into her life. Her impulse to seek common ground with figures situated in other centuries and countries and her focus on the long-standing identity of women as those who "help" are equally intriguing. Her project speaks to the value of looking for connections beyond one's immediate context, as well as to the power of enduring features in social landscapes.

Brown's "Order of the Scroll" is my inspiration for this chapter. I seek to assemble a collection of historically diverse young women to discern enduring patterns in how girls learn to read and write and what uses they make of these talents. In sweeping through the decades and across the nation, I do not mean to elide the important differences in the material, economic, cultural, and social circumstances of a girl living in Kansas City in 1911, for example, and a girl living in New York in 2011. I recognize that nuanced, close-in studies of specific groups of girls in particular historical and geographic contexts—studies like those offered by subsequent chapters in this volume—are essential for filling in crucial details on the intellectual maps by which we navigate. My goal, however, is to highlight the abiding features of girls' worlds, features so obvious and commonplace that they risk becoming part of the background scenery often unnoticed. I begin by offering a brief history of literacy instruction in U.S. high schools, before turning to four spatial imaginaries— the classroom, the extracurricular worlds of high school girls, the underlife of school where girls challenge authorities, and the worlds beyond school that invite girls to use literacy skills in a variety of satisfying ways. In these spaces, I will introduce you to the members of my "Order of the Scroll."

A Brief History of English in American High Schools

First appearing in secondary curricula between 1886 and 1890, "English"—a subject that combines grammar, writing/rhetoric and Anglo-American literature—has been a component of the academic experiences of adolescent girls in the U.S. for roughly 125 years (Applebee 37). Sketching the history of English instruction since the late nineteenth century is, however, no simple task. As Arthur N. Applebee notes, the history of English as a secondary school subject is "almost limitless" (ix), having been affected by shifts in moral philosophies and epistemologies, internecine scholarly battles over disciplinary identities, demographic shifts, the unstable flow of economic resources, and other factors. Turning one's historical gaze from macro-level issues to the micro-level of classroom practices presents other challenges. Instead of an easily plotted story of pedagogical innovation and educational achievement, teachers' documents and classroom artifacts tell a complex, recursive narrative. Through the decades, teachers have both embraced and resisted educational policymakers; they have resurrected discredited pedagogical approaches; and they have creatively responded to the material circumstances of their schools and students. Given these challenges, any historical sketch of English will fall short of being comprehensive and must acknowledge its own interestedness. Because my interests lie in how girls experience English classes and respond to school through literacy performances, the historical sketch offered here considers a key tension in English instruction: Should high school English classes focus on a body of culturally significant texts and the skills deemed necessary for college/career or should students' own interests and goals have priority?

In the late nineteenth century, teachers in the earliest incarnations of the modern high school would have found the idea of placing student interests at the center of their lesson plans quite curious. Instead, secondary curriculums were generally determined by reading lists of canonical literature on which the entrance exams of East Coast colleges were based. Typically, students composed essays on a literary work as evidence of their mastery of grammatical and rhetorical principles. Between 1886 and 1900, some of the most popular texts taught in high schools included plays by Shakespeare, Webster's "First Bunker Hill" oration, and poetry by Lowell, Longfellow, and Whittier, to name just a few (Applebee 36).

Though girls were limited in their opportunities to take entrance exams and pursue post-secondary educational opportunities, they were outnumbering boys in English classes by three to two at the turn of the twentieth century (Applebee 37). This may be partially due to the legacy of nineteenth-century female academies and finishing schools, where the ability to converse about *belles-lettres* was considered an appropriately feminine accomplishment (Applebee 13). The gendered nature of the English classroom at the turn of the century also reflected larger demographic trends in American education. According to Jane H. Hunter, "about 60 percent of the students in public high schools were girls" in 1900 (170), and they remained in the majority in most high schools throughout the first half of the twentieth century (Schrum 13). Hunter posits that the ability to send a daughter to high school—and to forgo any income from her labor—was increasingly seen as a sign of middle-class respectability (170).

These and other demographic trends, along with educators' growing frustration with the dominance of the uniform lists, created opportunities for the interests and experiences of adolescents to enter English classrooms, and educational goals other than college preparation were legitimized. Writing in 1903, high school principal Percival Chubb articulated two key factors teachers should consider in planning English classes:

> first, the characteristics, the needs, and the interests of the adolescent period; and secondly, the vocational and social demands made upon High School education. ... Education cannot simply be for power and for general culture; it must likewise be a novitiate for life, and must clear an opening into the vocations. (239–40)

To appeal to "the characteristics, the needs, and the interests of the adolescent period," teachers deployed a number of strategies in the first half of the twentieth century. They began introducing periodicals and popular novels into the classroom, and stage plays and school newspapers became more common. The arrival of radio and motion pictures in the 1920s and 1930s created other opportunities for tapping into students' interests. Kelly Schrum credits Edgar Dale's 1933 bestseller *How to Appreciate Motion Pictures* with spurring a national movement to teach film analysis, and in 1934 *Scholastic* magazine issued pamphlets for high school students entitled "How to Judge Motion Pictures" and "How to Organize a Photoplay Club" (131). Other teachers appealed to adolescent interests by having students define projects to take them beyond the classroom. Writing in the *English Journal* in 1947, George H. Henry describes a group of "noncollege-bound" pupils who explored the "colored question" in Dover, Delaware. The students reviewed statistical research, wrote letters, conducted interviews, and toured "the state college for colored students, where colored professors showed them around—the first time our students had even talked with Negroes better educated than themselves" (360). Ultimately, the students presented their findings at a school assembly and "were treated like authorities" (360).

To provide "an opening into the vocations" called for by Chubb and other Progressive reformers, many schools introduced differentiated courses of study. The standard curriculum that prepared students for college now competed with new "tracks"—Commercial, Manual Training, Art, Domestic Science. Along with courses in stenography, bookkeeping, and typing, a girl who opted for the Commercial track might write business letters, memos, and advertisements, rather than literary essays. A young woman enrolled in Domestic Science might debate whether "the virtues of Apple Sauce far surpass those of Banana Oil," rather than study the rhetorical precepts of Aristotle or Quintilian (Graves 282). Literary study across all tracks became largely instrumental as teachers sought to connect canonical literature to students' experiences and life goals. As Dorothy E. Moulton notes, by 1935 "the recognized leaders of teachers of English had declared their allegiance ... to progressivism rather than conservative principles in the teaching of literature" (60).

While the interests of adolescents first entered the English curriculum in the early decades of the twentieth century and remained a dominant force through the 1950s, increasingly there were calls for a return to the perceived rigor of the "great books" tradition meant to expose students to a common cultural heritage. The launch of Sputnik in 1957 and a spate of studies and articles in the popular press decrying the sad state of American education (e.g., Rudolf Flesch's *Why Johnny Can't Read* [1955]) fueled national concerns about educational and technological complacency. After surveying high school English textbooks in 1963, James Lynch and Bertrand Evans lamented that there was a general "fear of difficulty" and "deliberate catering to the adolescent mind":

> Pieces are chosen because they lie within the narrow boundaries of the teen-age world. ... The 'image' of the American Boy that emerges is of a clean-cut, socially poised extrovert, an incurious observer of life ... a willing conformer ... not much above a moron. And the 'image' of the American Girl? She is the one who likes the American Boy. (412–13)

Along with reclaiming a place for traditional literary study in the secondary class-room, English educators dissatisfied with a curricular focus on the interests and life adjustments of adolescents embraced a number of "new" theories of grammar and rhetoric that promised easily teachable structures and systems to ensure students would become increasingly competent language-users as they advanced through the grades (Parker 35). "The English curriculum reformers of the decade 1957–66," though, were, according to Robert Parker, "hardly reformers at all. Because their fundamental attitudes toward children, language, learning, and the English curriculum went back more than a hundred years, they were very much traditionalists, perhaps even reactionaries" (36).

This resurgence of the literary tradition and the focus on discrete language skills were challenged in 1966 by British and American teachers at the Dartmouth Conference. According to Parker, the British educators in attendance were less interested in defining English as an academic discipline and instead asked what English teachers do best (36). In a parallel move, the conference attendees shifted from discussing students as vehicles in which to deposit knowledge and instead conceived of them as individuals bringing their own linguistic habits and expertise into the classroom. Instead of a focus on exposing students to a literary canon or imparting particular skills to them, conference attendees concerned themselves with "activities and processes of learning ... rather than on the organization of knowledge into static forms to be received and mastered" (Parker 36). Classroom practices such as reading/writing workshops, opportunities to draft and revise essays and other assignments, peer response groups, and daily journal writing grew out of the Dartmouth Conference.

Arthur N. Applebee and Judith A. Langer's "A Snapshot of Writing Instruction in Middle Schools and High Schools" (2011) confirms that many of the ideals of the Dartmouth Conference have taken deep root among contemporary English teachers. Though high school students typically still compose brief texts with the teacher as the primary audience, over ninety percent of the English teachers in Applebee and Langer's study "spend class time generating and organizing ideas or information before writing" and "teach specific strategies for planning, drafting, revising and organizing written work" (20).

Teachers' abilities to implement rich, engaging literacy curricula for secondary students in the twenty-first century have been seriously constrained by the advent of high-stakes testing, most notably the passage of No Child Left Behind in 2001. As Applebee and Langer note: "Given the constraints imposed by high-stakes tests, writing as a way to study, learn, and go-beyond—as a way to construct knowledge or generate new networks of understandings ... is rare" (26). The impact of constant assessments on students' in-school reading has been equally detrimental. Milken award-winning teacher Sarah L. Crump argues:

> High-stakes testing and accountability have contributed to the literary famine seen in many secondary classrooms. ... [M]any teachers ... feel pressure and even fear for their jobs if their students don't perform well on standardized tests. ... Such concerns result in instruction that focuses on test preparation and quick improvement in scores rather than on constructs that are not easily measured but vitally important, such as motivation for reading and developing life-long readers. (33)

Currently, canonical literature and reading geared to adolescents' particular interests are likely presented to students as opportunities to practice the literacy skills demanded by high-stakes assessments.

What the future holds for girls in high school English classes remains to be seen. Professional educators such as Crump are increasingly vocal as they bring their expertise to bear in public conversations about literacy. Their voices are a positive force for minimizing the impact of high-stakes testing and instead creating a culture of schooling that supports girls as they learn to use language to cope with the increasingly complex, ever changeable world. As we begin to perceive the outlines of such a future for literacy education, listening to girls' voices from the past can be enlightening.

Learning to Read and Write in School

Whether girls encounter secondary English curricula that expose them to revered texts or that place adolescent interests at the center of study, evidence suggests that many girls always have been able to meet and surpass expectations. At her high school commencement exercises in St. Paul, Minnesota, in 1897, Mabel Stoughton read her literary essay "The Art of Arts." Her classmate, Caroline Polly Bullard, noted in her diary that Stoughton's essay "was the success of the evening. The applause was great, and she was called back again to bow" (Bunkers 89). Eighteen years later, Midwesterner Frances C. Royster composed a vivid sketch of her experience of "surf bathing" in response to an English assignment:

> Urged by the undertow I moved out farther where the giant waves did not break. As each mountain welled up before me, I rode easily over it, ascending high, then descending into a valley as the surf broke furiously into a mass of churning, bubbling, spraying, laughing, milk-white foam behind me.

Mabel Davis, who attended the Genoa Indian School in Nebraska in 1915, wrote an essay on "Cotton," detailing its history as a crop first mentioned by Herodotus, current methods of cultivation, and the uses of cotton "in the homes of both rich and poor" (210). As Amy M. Goodburn notes, Davis's essay reflects her ability to adapt to the demands of the federal boarding school system in which Native American students took academic classes in the morning and pursued vocational studies in the afternoon. Davis segues smoothly from historical research to a discussion of the uses of cotton in everyday garments, such as the apron she made and wore in her domestic science classes (94).

For Pat Huyett, who graduated from high school in Kansas in 1969, her most exciting writing assignment arose in her psychology class and seems to echo the type of project George H. Henry assigned his students in Delaware in the 1940s. Huyett decided to study the impact of socio-economic status within her high school. Writing in her diary, Huyett sounds exuberant:

> Absolutely fantastic. I am planning a fabulous psych term paper, and my tea-cher is very excited about it. It's going to be a research paper on the social

strata of the school. I plan to take 500 surveys (approx. 20% to 50% of the student body). I'm going to interview half the teaching staff (50) and then I'll interview representative and non-representative students of these groups. (14 November 1968)

More recently, high school sophomore Samantha Curfman authored her own impressive essay reflecting the work she and her classmates accomplished in the 2009/10 school year as they researched how to establish a student-led writing center. Arguing that a writing center serves students with a range of literacy skills, Curfman taps into the ethos of Martin Luther King, Jr. and Caesar Chavez, marshals statistics on educational attainment in urban schools, and shares her own experiences. Realizing, though, the need to persuade school administrators, she addresses how a writing center might improve performance on high-stakes tests. She offers this pertinent example:

> After discovering in a review that their district's writing instruction was inadequate, Wisconsin's New London school district began implementing a system of change. ... With careful budgeting, several [writing centers] were built in junior high and elementary schools, and the success of the centers inspired the district to open a writing center in the senior high in 1985. Student use, faculty interest, and administrative support were proven to be successful, and scores ... improved dramatically in the following years. The percentage of students scoring at or above grade level in 1987 was 73%, compared to 43% in 1982 (Behm). (69)

Mabel Stoughton, Frances Royster, Mabel Davis, Pat Huyett, and Samantha Curfman demonstrate that many girls are engaged by school writing assignments and are quite capable of achieving success in them.

Often, though, girls have not consistently complied with teachers' generic expectations, expressing instead transgressive opinions and views. As Goodburn has observed, while Mabel Davis' essay on "Cotton" celebrates agricultural models imported to North America by Western Europeans, a voice of resistance is found in the writing of one of Davis' classmates. Goodburn quotes the essay of Rosalie Sherman, who "traced the history of the English people from their earliest barbarous days to the present" and critiqued the high failure rate of federal Indian boarding schools by noting that just over fifty percent of her classmates earned diplomas (94–95). Julia Alvarez, who immigrated to the U.S. from the Dominican Republic, is also critical of the education she received in the early 1960s at Abbot Academy. She writes:

> My Abbot education not only put me in conflict with my parents and mi cultura, it put me in conflict with myself. I did not know how to integrate the competing selves inside me. What models were there for women in my family who had done this? What models were there of Hispanic women

doing this? ... The books we read—the canonical texts by white British and American mostly male writers—were no help to me either. (182–83)

Pat Huyett too expresses frustration with her English classes:

Mrs. B– and I do not agree when it comes to creative writing. I hand her a minor masterpiece, just dripping with professionalism and what does she scribble on it? A 94! Because I used both 1st and 2nd person in it. My theme on rain was beautiful, I thought. After giving me a 98 on a play report which was largely a bunch of quotes any way! (23 March 1967)

A year later Huyett continues to lament: "Sometimes I really hate school. I mean, there's such a system. ... English was horrible. My teacher always gave us tests with questions like 'What colour were Young Goodman Brown's wife's hat ribbons?' Symbolic meaning!" (23 January 1968).

While girls have critiqued their English assignments in memoirs, diaries, and other texts, they also have deliberately subverted the institutional structures of schooling. A student at Central High School in St. Louis just after the turn of the twentieth century, Fannie Hurst hoped to be the student speaker at commencement exercises. When called to the principal's office, though, it was not to receive accolades. The principal announced that a "surprising situation" had arisen, and he queried Fannie about how many compositions she had written for her classmates. Hurst acknowledged: "I stood accused and guilty. I wrote their compositions, I half explained, because it was difficult for them and easy for me." She and the classmates who had benefited from her skillful pen work were allowed to graduate, but without honors (78). Pat Huyett escaped punishment for a similar offense decades later. In one of her final diary entries documenting her high school career, she writes: "Blah-ness has set in. Got some hash and $2 for doing Brunk's term paper" (15 May 1969).

Scholars, teachers, researchers, parents, and other adults should heed the voices of girls like Rosalie Sherman, Julia Alvarez, Fannie Hurst and Pat Huyett, as these girls confirm the findings of Pamela J. Bettis and Natalie G. Adams, who note that girls have significant "disregard to the formal curriculum of the school in terms of defining themselves" (1). If educators are interested in making the formal curriculum more meaningful to girls, strategies need to be developed for reading between the lines of the written work they turn in and more formal feedback mechanisms need to be created so girls can share their reactions to the curriculum in spaces more public than diaries and more current than memoirs.

Extracurricular Literacy Lessons: Clubs, School Newspapers, and Yearbooks

Extracurricular opportunities for language learning have been an important feature of schools since the nineteenth century (Applebee 12). In literary societies and debating clubs, students might determine what texts they wish to read and what issues to take up; likewise, school newspapers and yearbooks serve as venues for students to share writing and ideas with wider audiences. Indeed, girls have often relished the sense of freedom that extracurricular activities afford them. Florence Wolfeson, attending New York City's Wadleigh High School for the Performing and Visual Arts in 1927, identified herself as a "literary Owlette" and learned to smoke in the basement office of the school newspaper office (Koppel 102). For Pat Huyett, working on the student newspaper in middle school gave her a chance to be in the school library after hours, where she "eaves-dropped on Student Council meetings ... looked at the sex manuals or ... read all the old magazines" (10 November 1966).

Such extracurricular activities typically exist, though, as liminal spaces where girls have a greater sense of self-direction even as they remain under the surveillance of school authorities. Polly Caroline Bullard, a sixteen-year-old in St. Paul, Minnesota, in 1897, writes enthusiastically of the new "literary academy" started at her school and the opportunity to discuss poets like the flamboyant Joaquin Miller; however, it is clear that this new club will be influenced by teachers: "The names are proposed for membership by the faculty, and chosen from among those whom they consider to be the brightest members of the school" (Bunkers 84). Some ninety years later, the High School Forensic Association was a significant "literacy sponsor" for Barbara Hunt, a student in rural Wisconsin (Brandt 39). Hunt competed in declamation, which involves memorizing and reciting dramatic pieces, and in the delivery of brief speeches she wrote herself (Brandt 39). Though an extracurricular activity, Hunt's participation in forensics was, as Deborah Brandt has noted, supervised by a certified coach and shaped by handbooks, instructional guides, and the competition rules of the statewide affiliate of the National Forensics Association (39).

Yearbooks and newspapers are also textual spaces where the institutional authority of teachers and principals seems to override any communicative agenda that students might have. The exquisite, hand-drawn 1900 yearbook of the Southern Home School (SHS) in Maryland contains a poem by Mavin Jamison, Nettie Jones, and Nannie Jones that celebrates "A Model Girl of the S.H.S." who is "exceeding studious," who has "studied French and English," and "been admired in every role from first to last." While the three co-authors articulate the values of their alma mater and what it means to be an ideal SHS girl, in the last stanza the "model girl" tearfully admits: "I met my fate last summer, I really did you see / I'm awfully in love with him, and he's in love with me" (Southern Home School Yearbook 13–14). By giving voice only in the final stanza to the romantic inclinations that distract them from the goals set forth by their teachers, the three co-authors structured their poem to reinforce the cultural logic that requires a choice between academic aspirations and heterosexual desires that lead to matrimony and motherhood.

In her analyses of yearbooks published at a segregated high school between 1915 and 1930, Henrietta Rix Wood documents the nuanced ways in which girls both celebrate their school and criticize the larger white society for racist educational policies. Wood cites Hazel Hickum, who published an honorific poem in *The Lincolnian* in 1917: "In Lincoln High, with pen and ink, / Our happiest days are spent / The teachers trained our minds to think / And we were all content" (175). Another Lincoln student, Willa Shaw, published a yearbook essay that catalogues the significant accomplishments of African-Americans, including W.E.B. DuBois and Alain Locke, and then derides the white press for biased coverage of the African-American community (Wood 205–06). Presumably, both Hickum's celebratory verses and Shaw's carefully modulated protests against racism would have met with the approval of the Lincoln faculty.

Girls who use extracurricular publications to explore more controversial subjects seem all too aware of the consequences of their writing. On January 17, 1967, Pat Huyett noted in her diary:

> I submitted my story 'Birthday Candle' to *Mektoub*, the school magazine. I hope it's considered. If they don't print it, I'll understand because it's about abortion and might not be considered appropriate. However if it *is* published it will no doubt make some kind of talk.

Huyett never documented whether "Birthday Candle" was published, but Lauren Obermark, a high school newspaper editor in the 1990s, had a very difficult experience. Though Lauren and her male co-editor had comic intentions when they finalized cartoons accompanying editorials on the different perspectives boys and girls bring to romantic relationships, school administrators confiscated all copies of the newspaper, and the faculty sponsor of the newspaper was dismissed from her teaching position. Reflecting on the experience several years later, Obermark noted: "I didn't trust what I wrote any more. Everything I wrote could cause disaster."

For many girls, opportunities to participate in literary clubs or activities like forensics, debates and yearbook are exciting and rewarding. What may be most important to remember about these sites is that they seem to function as compensatory spaces where girls gain some authority, even as adults ultimately exert control— either explicitly or implicitly. Those who work with girls should think and talk more explicitly with them about the limits of their abilities to claim discursive authority in these extracurricular spaces. The experiences of girls such as Pat Huyett and Lauren Obermark suggest that these conversations are overdue.

The Literacy Underlife at School

The types of textual performances required of students in classes and the opportunities to expand literacy repertoires through school-sanctioned extracurricular activities are certainly significant, but, as Margaret Finders documents, some of girls' most creative and impassioned work as readers and writers emerges when researchers shift their gaze to the literacy underlife of a school. For Finders, the literacy underlife refers to "those practices that refuse in some way to accept the official view, practices designed and enacted to challenge and disrupt the official expectations" (24).

Over the past hundred years and more, girls have found ample opportunities to write letters, compose jingles, pass notes, and use clothing to communicate with peers, teachers, and other members of school communities. In 1881, Mamie Greble violated the norms at St. Mary's Academy in South Bend, Indiana. Fellow student Etta Luella Call recorded in her diary on November 25:

> Oh! What terrible things will happen! ... Mother Lucretia came into the study hall and said that Mamie Greble had been expelled. What a silence fell upon the school! Mamie, the favorite of all the scholars, gone! She was expelled for corresponding with a boy whom she had never seen. ... This ought to be an example to the other girls and teach them not to put such confidence in boys, for the boy whom Mamie wrote to showed the sisters the letters himself. (Bunkers 67)

Fannie Hurst "wrote jingles about various teachers, passing them during study hall among the snickering students" (50). Julia Baskin, Lindsey Newman, Sophie Pollitt-Cohen, and Courtney Toombs passed a black-and-white composition notebook among themselves during their freshman year at Stuyvesant High School in Manhattan. These twenty-first century teens discussed their sexual explorations with boys and other girls, wrote about smoking marijuana and drinking alcohol, debated the politics of the Middle East, worried about high-stakes exams, and documented their participation in various activist causes, such as the Day of Silence in support of LGBTQ youth and protests against the Iraq war. In her final entry in the shared journal, Newman writes:

> The notebook is something that has helped me grow and change in the last three years more than anything else in my life. It has become a beloved fifth friend and a place that I could bring all of myself and all my baggage and be a better person for it. I have to say it's been liberating. Not to mention the crazy communication skillz [sic] we got from this whole experience. Every disagreement we have is talked through and resolved. It's weird that we never really fight, and every argument we have is resolved before we part. ... Despite all the drama, the real value of this notebook is apparent to me now more than ever. Being able to reflect on your life and yourself in this unique way is amazing. (24 December 2004)

Rather than passing a composition notebook among her friends, Madaline Walter-McCrary opted for a more overt literacy performance to disrupt the status quo at her suburban high school. She wore a white t-shirt with black lettering—"I like girls that like girls."—on the first day of her freshman year. Her school wardrobe included t-shirts with other important statements as well: "Legalize Gay, Repeal Prop 8" and "I have Lezb friends" (Bauer 16). By tapping into the discursive affordances of clothing, Walter-McCrary made a significant statement about her values and identity. As this example illustrates, the passion and energy that typically accompany girls' communicative activities when they author their own identities and engage in projects that resist official school culture suggest much about their willingness to embrace language as a source of power in their lives.

Beyond School Walls

While educational researchers, teachers, and parents are rightly focused on the literacy activities associated with school, girls have eloquently written about powerful literacy experiences in libraries, at the theater, in bookstores, and with friends. A variety of textual worlds beyond the school walls beckon to girls and provide important intellectual sustenance.

Born in the Warsaw ghetto in 1912, Kate Simon immigrated to the U.S. as a young girl. She could be precocious and self-directed in her reading at the public library:

> I went on the day of my graduation from elementary school to change my child's library card for one that permitted me to use the downstairs rooms for adults. ... Where the titles came from I don't know but I had ready a mental list of books to take from the adult shelves. ... [I]t was a proud thing to be turning the pages of such great thoughts and emotions. (175–76)

In the 1970s, Louisiana native Margaret Sartor also resorted to libraries as a space of physical comfort and intellectual sustenance. She writes: "[s]itting in a comfy chair in the library in the summer with the AC on is like sitting in a cloud" (233).

For other young women, commercial establishments provide important access to literacy resources. A 1948 alumna of Vassar College wrote about seeking answers to questions about her sexual identity as an adolescent, though she does not reveal where she accessed her reading material as a girl: "I had known the facts of sex from an early age, read *Lady Chatterley's Lover* at 12, had a young man court me at 16, but none of this related to me." Once in college she found a text—at the bookstore—that affirmed her sense of self: "In my senior year I somehow got the clue that Djuna Barnes' book *Nightwood* might be of interest. I bought a copy at the Co-op, went down to the small bridge at Sunset Lake and sat riveted through the whole story" (MacKay 26). Bookstores also figured in the literacy lives of Lindsey Newman and her friends:

> On Friday Courtney, Sophie, and I had a bonding experience in Barnes & Noble. We picked up sex books and magazines—it was fun. After reading the

joys of Kama Sutra it was on to sex for dummies by the really old lady who looks like the kid from Jerry McGuire [*sic*].

Theater is also an important sponsor of literacy activities for girls. On January 27, 1912, Dorothy Brown recorded several lines of dialogue from a production of *Julius Caesar*, starring Robert Mantell. A few weeks later, she saw a stage production of *Rebecca of Sunnybrook Farm*. In four sittings spread over ten days, Brown wrote 57 pages in her diary, summarizing the plot and commenting on the actors' performances. In the 1930s, Florence Wolfeson's love of theater was inspired in part by her admiration of Eva Le Gallienne, an actress and founder of the Civic Repertory Theatre in New York. Wolfeson went to see Le Gallienne's productions of Ibsen, Chekhov, and Shakespeare (Koppel 110) and was inspired to read the plays on her own. As Lily Koppel notes: "Florence wrote in her diary, 'Reading *Hedda Gabler* for the tenth time'" (115).

Many girls perform literacy activities through community organizations. Kate Stuart has studied the minutes kept by Jeanne Rataczak, secretary for the Beta Phi Theta Rho club in Joplin, Missouri, in the late 1940s. This organization for high school girls was affiliated with the International Order of Odd Fellows and International Rebekah Assemblies, both social service organizations. Stuart demonstrates that Rataczak used the power of her pen and the club minute book to establish her identity within the club and to limit the social authority of other girls. More recently, Mollie Blackburn has documented the range of literacy skills developed and deployed by adolescents as they participated in the governance of a community center serving queer youth.

For still other girls, friends and neighbors serve as informal teachers and expand their reading/writing worlds. Fannie Hurst frequently visited the basement retreat of Mr. Cleveland, a former college professor and husband of the owner of the boarding house in which Hurst's family lived. Hurst notes:

> It was in Mr. Cleveland's dark cave that I first encountered the name Plutarch. … From those same shelves Lecky's *History of European Morals* and Gibbon's *Decline and Fall of the Roman Empire* soared above my head like skyscrapers. … Novels were there too. … *David Copperfield*, *Père Goriot*, *The Scarlet Letter*. (59)

Pat Huyett enjoyed extended conversations with Linda, the older sister of her best friend, Diane. Linda attended Stanford University, and Pat sought opportunities to talk with her. Pat's diary entry on August 10, 1966, reads:

> Diane went to sleep but Linda and I stayed up and talked. She told me about Kafka and how she knew a lot of LSD users. We talked about literature, alchohol [*sic*], drugs, homosexuality, contraceptives, promiscuity, religion, dreams, and school. We talked until 3:00 in the morning.

Libraries, bookstores, theaters, organizations, neighbors, and friends have all created opportunities for girls to acquire and extend their skills as readers and writers. Religious organizations, workplaces, and countless other spaces beyond schools also stand as important sites of literacy education for girls. Exploring the enduring power of such sites of informal literacy education raises new questions about the scope and limits of the educational opportunities available to girls in schools.

Considerations

The young women introduced here—Mabel Davis and Samantha Curfman, Hazel Hickum and Pat Huyett, Fannie Hurst and Madaline Walter-McCrary, and all the others—stand as members of the "Order of the Scroll" that I imagine for myself as a scholar and teacher interested in girls and their literacies. Their reading and writing lives have an enduring relevance for me, just as Joan of Arc, Maid Marian, and Queen Victoria were relevant to Dorothy Allen Brown. While closely probing the nuanced lives of girls in a specific place and time can do much to advance understandings of how girls use words to engage with the particular worlds in which they are situated, so too is there value in looking for commonalties across time and circumstance. Bringing into view long-standing patterns in girls' literacy lives opens up questions about the abiding structures of educational institutions and entrenched assumptions about what it means to be young and female. For example, how have discourses of failure and crises repeatedly re-shaped literacy education and how might discourses of success and celebration change how we approach the perceived limitations of literacy instruction for girls in schools? What roles should extracurricular activities play in girls' lives and what lessons are girls learning about literacy, gender, and power as they participate in literary clubs, debating societies, school newspapers, and yearbooks? How might conversations about formal schooling be altered in light of the rich, informal learning opportunities that are so powerful in many girls' lives? A panoramic view of the history of girls' literacies adds to the urgency of pursuing such questions, and as researchers, educators, parents, and other advocates for girls take up such questions, we help create the possibility that strong, smart girls with literacy skills we have yet to imagine will be future candidates for an "Order of the Scroll" in which we can all be proud members.

Acknowledgments

LaBudde Special Collections Department in UMKC's Miller-Nichols Library was tremendously helpful in directing me to many of the documents referenced. I'm particularly grateful to Stuart Hinds and Teresa Gipson. Henrietta Rix Woods, Alexandra Ledgerwood and Kate Stuart gave helpful feedback on this chapter. And a very heartfelt thanks to Pat Huyett for donating her rich, rollicking girlhood diaries to UMKC's library and for being such a positive presence in the lives of her students and colleagues through the years.

Works Cited

Alvarez, Julia. *Once upon a Quinceañera: Coming of Age in the USA*. New York: Plume, 2007. Print.

Applebee, Arthur N. *Tradition and Reform in the Teaching of English: A History*. Urbana, IL: NCTE, 1974. Print.

Applebee, Arthur N. and Judith A. Langer. "A Snapshot of Writing Instruction in Middle Schools and High Schools." *English Journal* 100.6 (July 2011): 14–27. Print.

Baskin, Julia, Lindsey Newman, Sophie Pollitt-Cohen, and Courtney Toombs. *The Notebook Girls*. New York: Warner, 2006. Print.

Bauer, Laura. "Behind the Color Barrier: These Teens Feel Judged by Their Race or Culture, But They're Comfortable in Their Own Skin." *Kansas City Star Magazine*, 27 Feb. 2011: 6–18. Print.

Bettis, Pamela J. and Natalie G. Adams. "Landscapes of Girlhood." *Geographies of Girlhood: Identities In-Between*. Eds. Pamela J. Bettis and Natalie G. Adams. Mahwah, NJ: Lawrence Erlbaum Associates, 2005. 1–16. Print.

Blackburn, Mollie. "Exploring Literacy Performances and Power Dynamics at The Loft: Queer Youth Reading the World and the Word." *Research in the Teaching of English* 37 (2003): 467–69. Print.

Brandt, Deborah. *Literacy in American Lives*. Cambridge: Cambridge UP, 2001. Print.

Brown, Dorothy Allen. "Diary." 1911. *Little Colonel's Goodtime Book*. University of Missouri, Kansas City Libraries, Dr. Kenneth J. LaBudde Special Collections Department. Print.

Bunkers, Suzanne, ed. *Diaries of Girls and Women: A Midwestern American Sampler*. Madison: University of Wisconsin Press, 2001. Print.

Chubb, Percival. *The Teaching of English in the Elementary and Secondary School*. New York: Macmillan, 1903. Print.

Crump, Sarah L. and Karen J. Kindle. "From Famine to Feast: Enriching Reading Instruction in Secondary Classrooms." *The Missouri Reader: Journal of the Missouri Reading Association* 35.2 (2011): 32–37. Print.

Curfman, Samantha. "The Impact of a Writing Center on an Inner-City High School." *Sosland Journal* 2009–10: 67–70. Print.

Davis, Mabel. "Cotton." *Indian News*, September 1915: 5–6. Reprinted in *Girls and Literacy in America: Historical Perspectives to the Present*. Ed. Jane Greer. Santa Barbara, CA: ABC-Clio, 2003. 207–10. Print.

Finders, Margaret J. *Just Girls: Hidden Literacies and Life in Junior High*. New York: Teachers College Press, 1997. Print.

Goodburn, Amy. "Girls' Literacy in the Progressive Era: Female and American Indian Identity at the Genoa Indian School." *Girls and Literacy in America: Historical Perspectives to the Present*. Ed. Jane Greer. Santa Barbara, CA: ABC-Clio, 2003. 79–101. Print.

Graves, Karen. *Girls' Schooling during the Progressive Era: From Female Scholar to Domesticated Citizen*. New York: Garland, 1988. Print.

Henry, George H. "Our Best English Unit." *English Journal* 36.7 (1947): 356–62. Print.

Hunter, Jane H. *How Young Ladies Became Girls: The Victorian Origins of American Girlhood*. New Haven, CT: Yale University Press, 2002. Print.

Hurst, Fannie. *Anatomy of Me: A Wonderer in Search of Herself*. Garden City, NY: Doubleday, 1957. Print.

Huyett, Patricia Lee. "Diaries." 1966–69. University of Missouri, Kansas City Libraries, Dr. Kenneth J. LaBudde Department of Special Collections. Print.

Koppel, Lily. *The Red Leather Diary: Reclaiming a Life through the Pages of a Lost Journal*. New York: Harper, 2008. Print.

Lynch, James J. and Bertrand Evans. *High School English Textbooks: A Critical Examination*. Boston, MA: Little, Brown, 1963. Print.

MacKay, Anne. *Wolf Girls at Vassar: Lesbian and Gay Experiences, 1930–1990*. New York: St. Martin's, 1992. Print.

Mason, James Hocker. "The Educational Milieu, 1874–1911: College Entrance Requirements and the Shaping of Secondary Education." *English Journal* 68.4 (1979): 40–45. Print.

Moulton, Dorothy E. "Years of Controversy in the Teaching of English." *English Journal* 68.4 (1979): 60–66. Print.

Obermark, Lauren. "High School Newspaper Trauma." 5 June 2009. Digital Archives of Literacy Narratives. http://daln.osu.edu/handle/2374.DALN/577, 26 June 2011. Web.

Parker, Robert. "From Sputnik to Dartmouth: Trends in the Teaching of Composition." *English Journal* 68.6 (1979): 32–37. Print.

Royster, Frances C. "Surf Bathing." Frances Royster Williams Collection (KC249). State Historical Society of Missouri Research Center, Kansas City, 1915. Print.

Sartor, Margaret. *Miss American Pie: A Diary of Love, Secrets, and Growing Up in the 1970s*. New York: Bloomsbury, 2006. Print.

Schrum, Kelly. *Some Wore Bobby Sox: The Emergence of Teenage Girls' Culture, 1920–1945*. New York: Palgrave Macmillan, 2004. Print.

Simon, Kate. *Bronx Primitive: Portraits of a Childhood*. New York: Viking, 1982. Print.

Southern Home School Yearbook, 1900. University of Missouri, Kansas City Libraries, Dr. Kenneth J. LaBudde Special Collections Department. Print.

Stuart, Kate. "Girls in Business Meetings: Beta Phi Theta Rho Secretaries Take Charge, 1946–50." *Young Scholars in Writing* 1 (2003): 7–24. Print.

Wood, Henrietta Rix. "Praising Girls: The Epideictic Rhetoric of Young Women, 1895–1930." Dissertation, University of Missouri, Kansas City, 2011. Print.

PART II
Girls Made Visible

2

TEACHING HISTORICALLY BASED, CULTURALLY RICH YA NOVELS WITH STRONG GIRL PROTAGONISTS

Linda J. Rice

Historical fiction and non-fiction for young adults offer a special opportunity for readers to explore, understand, and connect with different times, places, and cultures. Being immersed in history and culture through literature promotes opportunities for vicarious experiences while deepening human understanding. This chapter offers a brief overview of historically based, culturally rich novels that feature strong female protagonists. It is not that the girls in these stories were born strong; instead, they demonstrate their strength and resilience by learning to face complex and challenging situations, make difficult decisions, and persevere. It is important young people realize that, no matter how difficult their circumstances, purposefulness and determination can help them press forward and, in many cases, may enable them to overcome great hardship in ways beneficial to themselves and others. Oftentimes, such efforts impact the world in which we all live in a positive manner. Girls reading these books will be inspired by the possibilities presented and the concept of what it means to lead a self-determined life. All readers will see how the intelligence, innovation, resourcefulness, and will power of girls can be the pivot point for moving from despair to hope.

A variety of approaches may be taken when teaching literature meant to expand understandings of history and culture. A common method is to arrange books by era, subject, or conflict; for example, everyone might read a book or a group of books about the Great Depression and then move similarly to books about the Second World War. Another option is to organize books by nation or region. Dividing a class into groups where some students read stories set in South Africa, while others read stories set in Ghana, Sierra Leone, or Sudan, serves to highlight differences among African nations. Another organizing strategy is to arrange books by theme; this requires some work, but an advantage of the approach is that it highlights themes across different time periods and cultures. This chapter stands as an example of this approach and is organized according to four themes: Girls, Injustice and Personal Sacrifice; Girls in a World of Men; Political Ideologies and Girls; and Loss of Culture and Family. In addition to looking at historically and culturally focused books that highlight how girls must negotiate the world, several teaching strategies accompanied by creative student responses also follow. The suggested strategies can be adapted to any novel and include the Character-to-Self Artifact Connections Grid, a Futuristic Script, a Character Transformation through Charcoal Drawings, and Specialized Poetic Forms, in particular a Pantoum.

Girls, Injustice and Personal Sacrifice

Young Adult Literature (YAL) has long introduced readers to female characters willing to give up something of themselves for the betterment of others. Two classics that demonstrate this theme include *Number the Stars* (Lowry 1989), in which Annemarie Johansen helps the Rosen family escape the Nazis, and *Spite Fences* (Krisher 1994) the story of thirteen-year-old Maggie Pugh who uses her camera to document injustice during the time of American racial desegregation. A fitting parallel to Maggie Pugh, though in a different time and place, is the title character in *Lizzie Bright and the Buckminster Boy* (Schmidt 2004). Lizzie's story is one of determination to save Malaga Island, a poor fishing community of black, white, and mixed race people that is slated for evacuation so that a lucrative tourist trade can be established. More recent texts that offer students exposure to somewhat less familiar countries and histories include stories of girls in Sierra Leone, India, Sudan, and South Africa.

The Bite of the Mango (Kamara with McClelland 2008) chronicles the experience of growing up female in a small rural village in Sierra Leone that has been attacked by rebel soldiers. While Mariatu's physical and emotional journey is at times heart wrenching, her story is ultimately an inspiring one of courage and resilience. Different in its message, *Sold* (McCormick 2006) tells the story of Lakshmi, a girl from Nepal sold into sexual slavery in India by her father. While unable to confront the gross injustices done to her and the other girls at Happiness House, Lakshmi does hold on to the belief that her personal sacrifice will bring good to her family as she affords them money for a new roof and other material needs. That Lakshmi maintains hope in light of the most dire circumstances is a testament to the human spirit and the inner strength girls must often call upon to overcome incredible hardships. (It should be reiterated here that though *Sold* is a carefully researched work of fiction, one can only hope that girls like Lakshmi are able to persevere as she does while waiting for rescue.) Set in Sudan, *A Long Walk to Water* (Park 2010) tells the story of Nya and the sacrifices she makes for her family, while *Chanda's Wars* (Stratton 2004), a South African novel, is about a girl who risks everything to save her brother and sister.

It is important that students find a way to connect to these strong girls whose lives are so different from their own but who have so much to teach them about life. One way is to have them keep a record of artifacts valued by the characters, and then determine parallels from their own lives that connect them in more personal ways. An example of this strategy in response to *Sold* appears in Table 2.1. A group of pre-service teachers I worked with designed a project they called "Our Bundle." The students wrapped up personal artifacts in a piece of cloth reminiscent

TABLE 2.1 Our Bundle: Character-to-Self Artifact Connections Grid (Chelsie Arrowood, Theresa Evans and Leah Stoltzfus)

Item from Book	What It Means to Lakshmi	Your Symbolic Item	How It Relates
Piece of a Tin Roof: Something that reminds you of your ultimate goal	What I want for my mother. I am willing to travel to a strange city to work to get this for my family.	Coaster with "To teach is to touch a life forever" quote	My ultimate goal is to become a teacher and this quote reminds me of the importance of the teaching profession.
David Beckham Shirt: An item that reminds you that there is good in the world	Harish wears a Beckham shirt and I am grateful for his kindness and his teachings.	Rural Action brochure	I worked with this organization through Americorp for two summers and love all the things they do for the local communities.
Children's Elmo Book: Something that makes you want to learn	My independence. I looked forward to my lessons with Harish every day so I could learn to read. Maybe it will help me in the future.	*Fall of the Roman Republic* by Plutarch	Anything that has to do with history spikes my curiosity and makes me want to learn as much as I can about the topic of the book. I especially love the history of the Roman Empire.
Business Card: Something that reminds you of a time you were befriended	The American came, not to have sex but to show that he wanted to help me, and he was my friend.	A "lucky coin"	This was from a customer at the bank where I worked. He was not a man to give anything away, and when he found out I was leaving for vacation, he gave me his lucky coin to take on the plane with me.
Piece of Fabric from My Skirt: Something from your childhood	My childhood was spent in one village surrounded by the same people. This skirt is from my life in the village.	Old Nintendo Game Boy with Dr. Mario	While in the car I would either bring this or a book to keep me occupied. My sister and I shared.

TABLE 2.1 (CONTINUED)

Item from Book	What It Means to Lakshmi	Your Symbolic Item	How It Relates
Rice, My Family's Income: Something that reminds you that life does have hard times	Growing rice is hard but so important to my family's well-being. Even though our yield isn't always high we have to do it.	Bubble bath bottle (Philosophy— Amazing Grace)	It has the passage written on it: "How you climb the mountain is just as important as how you get down the mountain and, so it is with life, which for many of us becomes one big gigantic test followed by one big gigantic lesson. In the end, it all comes down to one word. Grace. It's how you accept winning and losing, good luck and bad luck, the darkness and the light."
Pencil Harish Gave Me: Something that makes you have faith or belief	The smells of lead and rubber gave me a sense of hope and possibility.	Picture from my confirmation	My Mom brought us to church since we were little, and I was confirmed in the eighth grade.
Eucalyptus Leaf: Something that reminds you of home	This leaf grows on the trees in my home village in Nepal. My life was spent outside when I was in my village and this leaf reminds me of that.	Disney Refrigerator Magnet	Our family collects them, and our refrigerator is covered in them. It is something personal to our family and home.
Rupees: Something that reminds you that you will get there	For the journey home. I will get there.	One of Reagan's (my baby) toys	Even though the wait was long and sometimes stressful and full of worry, Reagan came, and she is wonderful.

of what the protagonist Lakshmi would have had and then charted the parallel meanings and relationship to Lakshmi. While the experiences are certainly worlds apart, an opening to understanding a character whose life and situation are so different is made palpable through the exercise. Important discussions can be generated by this simple but thoughtful activity, especially in regard to the injustices brought to light by books that expose issues impacting girls that are not commonly confronted but that adults well know exist. The items from the book and why they are so important to the characters can stimulate a variety of discussions.

Girls in a World of Men

Awareness of gender continues to pervade daily life in common ways such as the language we use, the clothes we wear, the roles we inhabit or the responsibilities we assume. While American culture has made great strides in gender equity in the past century, an examination of history at home and cross-culturally highlights ways girls and women live that remain patriarchal in nature or that require a degree of conformity in order to benefit socially or economically. Two classic examples of girls having to struggle in a man's world are *Behind Rebel Lines: The Incredible Story of Emma Edmonds, Civil War Spy* (Reit 1998) and *Nowhere to Call Home* (DeFelice 1999). Respectively set in the Civil War and the Great Depression, both novels feature female protagonists who must disguise themselves as men in order to contribute to and survive in the society in which they live.

More recent examples of girls having to navigate a patriarchal society include *Homeless Bird* (Whelan 2000), the story of Koly, a Hindu girl facing an arranged marriage, a tradition she longs to flee, and *Uncommon Faith* (Krisher 2003), the story of Faith Common, a bold young woman who in 1837 challenges the notion that women should limit their education and obediently perform domestic duties. Other examples of YAL that feature girls willing to fight for their right to be educated through a span of times and cultures are *Climbing the Stairs* (Venkatraman 2008), the story of fifteen-year-old Vidya who dreams of going to college, an unusual proposition for a girl living in British-occupied India during the Second World War, and *Firehorse* (Wilson 2006), in which strong-willed fifteen-year-old Rachel dreams of becoming a veterinarian during the time of the Great Boston Fire of 1872.

A book that deals with contemporary historical events is *In the Name of God* (Jolin 2007), which is set in the Middle East in the aftermath of 9/11. In Damascus, Syria, seventeen-year-old Nadia is influenced by her cousin's hard-line religious views (including the role of women) and political opinions. Drawn into Islamic Fundamentalism, Nadia agrees to become a suicide bomber. The book is believable and suspenseful and "creates an essential starting place for teens to examine their own views about Western culture, the Middle East, the division of church and state, terrorism, and how fear and hate, faith and love affect everything" (Engberg 38). This book is an excellent one to help students unpack the work girls must do to live in a world that has mostly been determined by men.

A teaching strategy meant to help students engage meaningfully with these kinds of texts and cultivate a deeper understanding of their pertinent issues, while utilizing their own creative natures, is the futuristic script. In this form of simulation or role-play, students imagine what happens after a book ends. They create a scene such as a skit or interview that they act out in front of the class to show something more about the characters and issues in the book. Table 2.2 presents an example of the futuristic script created by pre-service teacher Tessa Liniger as she imagined how *In the Name of God* protagonist Nadia would have changed after her near decision to end her life and destroy others as a suicide bomber.

TABLE 2.2 Futuristic Script (Tessa Liniger)

Cast:

Under-Secretary General and Executive Director of UN Women, Michelle Bachelet: Tessa

Samira: Paige

Nadia: Emma

Iraqi Delegate: Brian

American Delegate: Dave

Bachelet: Ladies and gentlemen, thank you for being here today for our panel on Women, War and Peace. Monday, March 8th, marked the passing of the 100th anniversary of International Women's Day, and today we will draw attention to the importance for continued celebration of women and stressing their role in our world. My name is Michelle Bachelet, and I am the Under-Secretary General for the UN as well as the Executive Director of UN Women. Our featured speakers today are two young women from Syria. Both have interned here in Geneva, and both have their own interesting perspective on the need to empower women. With that, I'll turn the table over to them.

Samira: Thank you, Ms. Bachelet. My name is Samira and, like Ms. Bachelet told you, I have recently interned here and have garnered so much knowledge regarding the UN's role in the empowerment of women. I am delighted to have discovered the Namibia Plan of Action on Mainstreaming a Gender Perspective—this document and the people supporting it have focused on supporting peace in a multidimensional way. This plan calls for women to be actively engaged in creating peace in their countries and implores world leaders, like you, to permit and support their efforts at all levels.

Coming from Syria, I have experienced some of the negative effects of being a woman in a religiously and politically patriarchal society. It's not easy to have a message and an opinion when those in power won't grant you so much as a chance to be heard because of your gender. My fellow intern, who also happens to be my cousin, can tell you a bit more about that frustration, though. So, Nadia if you'll share …

Nadia: Thanks Samira. My name is Nadia and, as Samira mentioned, I know the frustration of being silenced by your government. Just this summer, my cousin, and Samira's brother, Fowzi was arrested for his political views and actions against an oppressive government. It became clear to me then that, since our government wouldn't even tolerate a man speaking out against them, any claim I tried to make for free speech could be as potentially fatal as a suicide bomb. (Jolin, pp. 120–22, 124–25)

TABLE 2.2 (CONTINUED)

After that realization, listening to the radicals no longer seemed so fanatical, so bizarre. The fundamentalist radicals seemed willing to let women share their efforts to create peace by ridding the world of infidels. It seemed to make sense. Still, I was conflicted. I prayed and prayed, and it seemed to me the answer was to become a woman on a mission for God. From there, surprisingly quickly, clandestine meetings were set up between an ally of Fowzi's and myself. Knowing I was a woman and would never be suspected of aiding and abetting terrorists, he enlisted me to buy the components for a bomb. Which I did. With alarming ease. Then, after I had all the pieces I needed, it occurred to me that in life I would never have a voice in my country—but, in death, in martyrdom, I would. So, I asked to be the one.

Fortunately, I ran into a family member on the day of the scheduled detonation and the disruption he caused in my plan was long enough to let me think things through. It occurred to me that "religion requires a person to stretch herself with kindness, to make allowances, to seek out good in everyone" and, well, blowing myself up wouldn't accomplish that and wouldn't inspire others to do the same (207). Now I want to speak out for peace among all believers and ask governments around the world to ensure that women are granted equality—underestimating us can only be perilous, as my story will attest.

Bachelet: Thank you, ladies. You, I know, will be very successful in your endeavors to help women achieve peace and equality around the world. Now we will open the floor to any questions.

Iraqi Delegate: Hello, ladies. Thank you for sharing what you have learned here and at home. I am from Iraq, a Muslim country like yours, and I just wondered what you perceive to be practical steps towards change in countries such as ours that have long-standing and faith-based traditions regarding women?

Samira: Well, first I would encourage all world leaders to look at Resolution 1325 and adhere to some of the measures it suggests. This is a resolution specifically concerning issues faced by women the world over.

The most relevant issue in 1325 would be "stressing the importance of … equal participation and full involvement" of women in efforts to maintain peace as well as increasing the role of women in "decision-making with regard to conflict prevention and resolution." I know it might be uncomfortable considering the Quran's commandments for men to protect and preserve the virtue of women. But, and not trying to add to the scriptures here, it might help men to consider that allowing women a voice in how they will be treated by their governments and societies would be an invaluable step toward protecting them more thoroughly.

TABLE 2.2 (CONTINUED)

Nadia: I agree with Samira, but I would also say those leaders ought to consider what will come of casting people as villains when their only crime is to disagree—I had to. I had to ask myself honestly why I questioned Samira, others in my family, and a large portion of people in Damascus just because they didn't see the world closing in on them and their faith the way I did. I think there is a lot to be said for simply trying to see things from another's perspective. I agree that we have to be faithful to who we are nationally and if we profess a faith, we should do so sincerely. But it is important to bear in mind that just because "that's how it's always been done" doesn't mean that's how it should continue to be done.

I'm clearly more opinionated than Samira. Sorry if I offend anyone.

American Delegate: Nadia, can you tell us a little more about what stopped you that day and any advice you would give to a woman contemplating a suicide mission like you had?

Nadia: Well, I can tell you, "it is very strange to wake up on the last day of your life" (196). And I would advise those women to think about what they're dying for and be honest, even if it means being embarrassed by your own motivations. I know I was humbled and ashamed when I asked myself why I was ready to detonate a bomb in a tourist-packed hotel. I realized I was there to make history for myself, not bring glory to God. I was there to impress a man, not liberate my fellow believers or countrymen.

My advice to Islamic women, and women all over the world, would be to set your mind on living for a cause, not dying for one.

Bachelet: That's an excellent point Nadia. Thank you and Samira both for speaking with us today. Thank you for reminding us what the UN has accomplished in the way of protecting women's rights, and what work we've left to do. In 1934 Eleanor Roosevelt pointed out that people asked what women had done in the fourteen years since they gained the right to vote. "I often wonder," she said, "why they don't ask men the same question." Still, she deemed it a high compliment to women that they were expected to bring about change. And indeed, it is women themselves who, in the end, will bring about change in their own political condition. In the UN Women, they now have a steadfast, committed partner.

Thank you, ladies and gentlemen, for your time and attention. And again, Happy International Women's Day!

The setting for Tessa's futuristic script is the 100th anniversary of International Women's Day, when Michelle Bachelet, the Under-Secretary General and Executive Director of UN Women, convenes a panel on Women, War, and Peace. The panel includes Nadia, Nadia's cousin Samira, an Iraqi Delegate and an American Delegate. As readers of the script will note, Tessa addresses "the negative effects of being a woman in a religiously and politically patriarchal society" and advocates for "governments around the world to ensure that women are granted equality." She also references the Quran, warns of the danger of "casting people as villains when their only crime is to disagree," and urges women to set their mind on "living for a cause, not dying for one."

Tessa also incorporates independent research into her script, a valuable experience for students when studying a text of an unfamiliar culture or era. In particular, she references UN Resolution 1325, which addresses women in international conflict and their role in achieving and maintaining peace, and a speech by the UN Under-Secretary General that reports on the progress of women's rights. Tessa's script demonstrates a clear understanding of how Nadia's character evolves throughout the novel while foregrounding healthy ways that girls can be advocates of change.

Political Ideologies and Girls

The range of YAL featuring political conflicts across years and cultures is vast. Considering the scores of books written about the Holocaust over the past three decades, a whole chapter could be devoted to this topic alone. Among the particularly noteworthy and popular more recent works depicting the Holocaust are: *I Will Plant You a Lilac Tree: A Memoir of a Schindler's List Survivor* (Hillman 2005) and *The Book Thief* (Zusak 2005) which tells the story of Liesel, a young girl living outside Munich in Nazi Germany whose story tells how books help provide the strength to go on living in horrific times. Anne Frank's *The Diary of a Young Girl* (2005) still stands as the classic Holocaust text, written by a strong girl protagonist who must live and die by the political order of her world. While students are apt to be somewhat familiar with the Holocaust and even other politically driven issues such as America's history of slavery, as tackled in a book like *Hang a Thousand Trees with Ribbons: The Story of Phillis Wheatley* (Rinaldi 1996), they are probably less familiar with stories of tsarist Russia, living in wartime Iraq, or the effects of the Cold War on Americans. There are, however, some excellent novels about these topics that have strong female characters and will help readers gain a critical understanding of important historical events, eras, and issues and the roles girls have often played.

In *Angel on the Square* (Whelan 2001) Katya joins the family of Russian tsar Nikolai II when her mother becomes one of the empress's ladies-in-waiting. While not a member of the aristocracy herself, Katya has an insider's view of the crumbling of tsarist Russia from 1913 to 1918. In *Annie, Between the States* (Elliott 2004) Annie Sinclair's Virginia home is on the battle path of the Civil War, and she tends to injured soldiers while her brothers fight in the war. Annie falls in love with a Union lieutenant and, with a divided heart, must choose her own course. *Thura's Diary: My Life in Wartime Iraq* (Al-Windawi 2004) is a memoir that describes the author's upbringing in Iraq under "the repressive regime of Saddam Hussein in an atmosphere of secrecy and terror" (Al-Windawi, inside dust jacket), the intense bombing of Baghdad in 2003, and the hard pursuit of normalcy in the aftermath of war. Finally, *Fallout* (Krisher 2006) tells the story of Genevieve Hardcastle and her friend Brenda Wompers who, against the backdrop of the Cold War and Senator Joseph McCarthy's list of alleged communists, must navigate their differences and beliefs. It is this book that is the focus for another teaching approach.

Many strategies provide students with opportunities for hands-on and visual learning that foster creativity and promote deeper ways to connect with a literary text. Allowing students alternative ways to respond can make the reading experience more personally enjoyable. They might elect to create dioramas, mobiles, storyboards, or, as featured in Figures 2.1, 2.2 and 2.3, a set of charcoal drawings. Student Christine Madjar used charcoal drawings to respond to Krisher's *Fallout*. In the novel, fourteen-year-old Genevieve goes from being a shy, timid girl to a confident and brave one. While Christine could have chosen any medium to express her ideas, she decided on charcoal:

> The use of charcoal pencils is quite significant. The idea of black and white seems to be a reoccurring theme through the novel—one is either right or wrong about all issues. For example, the community of Easton shuns the Wompers for ideas that they believe are wrong. It reflects the quote, "If you are not with us, you are against us." However, most subjects are neither right or wrong nor black or white, but rather have a gray area. Thus, the drawings are all gray.

FIGURE 2.1 Character Transformation through Charcoal Drawings: Genevieve and Father

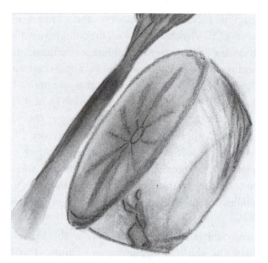

FIGURE 2.2 Genevieve Trapped

FIGURE 2.3 Genevieve and Kitten

Christine's project consists of three drawings and accompanying explanations. "From one drawing to the other," as stated in the essay accompanying the drawings, Christine was able to "convey a process that most adolescents must endure—finding one's self."

Loss of Culture and Family

As the themes thus far demonstrate, culturally rich YA novels featuring strong girl protagonists persevering, making sacrifices, overcoming political situations, or navigating harsh circumstances are not uncommon. This is equally the case in novels organized around the fourth and final theme: Loss of Culture and Family. History shows aggressors and conquerors, leaders and regimes that build power by squashing the thoughts and ideologies of competitors whether for political, religious, or cultural reasons. Classic works of YAL that exemplify this include *Song of the Buffalo Boy* (Garland 1992), *Red Scarf Girl* (Jiang 1997), and *Farewell to Manzanar* (Houston and Houston 1973). Dealing respectively with the plight of Amerasian children left in the aftermath of the Vietnam conflict, the Cultural Revolution in China, and Japanese internment camps, each of these texts shows the devastation that comes to individuals and families when they are denied the right to live in a manner that is true to their culture. Jiang's and Houston and Houston's true accounts depict families forcibly divided by government entities, thus magnifying the sense of loss.

There are also many more recent works available that span different times and nations while highlighting the loss of culture and family. Two books that would pair nicely with Jiang's classic *Red Scarf Girl* are *Little Green* (Yu 2005) and *Snow Falling in Spring* (Li 2008). *When My Name Was Keoko* (Park 2002) tells the story of Sun-hee and her brother Sookan as they are forced to suppress their Korean culture when the Japanese invade their country, and *Between Sisters* (Badoe 2010) tells the story of 16-year-old Gloria's move from Accra to Kumasi and the temptations, involving stepping away from family and traditional culture, that come with greater prosperity. Both *Keoko* and *Sisters* present common themes of the cultural struggles often faced by families in shifting circumstances. Finally, *My Name Is Sally Little Song* (Woods 2006) tells the story of Sally May Harrison, a slave who escapes to live in an Indian village where, though free, she must redefine her sense of family and adjust culturally.

Whether set in 1802 Georgia, USA, 1960s China, 1970s Vietnam, or present day Ghana, the YAL discussed in this section exemplifies determined girls who endure despite the powers that seek to take away their freedom and natural-born identity while demolishing the traditions they hold dear. The inspiring nature of these books does not shy away from harsh realities but positions readers to consider deeply what it means to be part of a family, to have traditions, and to, at least internally, maintain a moral compass that no outside force can dismantle.

Providing students with a range of specialized poetic forms they may choose from to write poems from a character's perspective is a final strategy for promoting deeper personal understanding and engagement with texts. Moving from relatively simple to quite complex, recommended specialized poetic forms that will challenge writers of varying interests and abilities include the Triolet (8 lines), Rondel (13–14 lines), Rondeau (15 lines), Villanelle (19 lines), Pantoum (indefinite number of quatrains), and Sestina (39 lines). Teachers will find explanations and examples of each of these poetic forms through a standard Internet search. Some forms have particular rhyme schemes or repeat certain lines or end words in a specified order.

TABLE 2.3 Pantoum with Accompanying Explanation for *My Name Is Sally Little Song* (Christina Stabile)

I keep singing my songs Though fear is always on my mind The heat of the sun keeps beating on my back And the days keep passing by slowly Though fear is always on my mind And my hands are raw from picking cotton And the days keep passing by slowly I hold to the hope of freedom and keep going And my hands are raw from picking cotton I keep my eyes low and my opinions to myself I hold to the hope of freedom and keep going This is life as a slave I keep my eyes low and my opinions to myself Family is the glue that holds me together This is life as a slave My hope is for freedom Family is the glue that holds me together The heat of the sun keeps beating on my back My hope is for freedom I keep singing my songs	When writing the Pantoum, I wanted the poem to be from the perspective of Sally. I thought that I could clearly communicate her perspective because of the fact that she is the one narrating the novel. As a reader I felt that I truly was able to understand where she comes from. Since the novel is broken into three sections, I decided that I would focus on one. Specifically, I wrote about the first part of the novel, which is Sally's experience on the plantation. The Pantoum begins and ends with the line "I keep singing my songs." I wanted these lines to be the main focus of the poem because singing songs is a part of who Sally is. Singing was what helped her cope with the many hardships she had to face. Working in the cotton fields is a clear example of how singing songs would help Sally get through the day. The poem explains Sally's daily struggles of living on the plantation. I wanted the reader of the poem to get a better glimpse of what it was like for Sally to have beatings from the master, having raw and bloody hands from picking cotton, and also the tight knit bond that Sally had with her family. I wanted this piece to be a personal experience between Sally and the reader.

Table 2.3 offers an example of a Pantoum written by student Christina Stabile in response to *My Name Is Sally Little Song*.

A Pantoum is made up of an indefinite number of quatrains of any length, but lines 2 and 4 of each stanza become lines 1 and 3 of the subsequent stanza. As the poem closes, it circles back to where it began with the last line repeating the first line of the poem, and the second line of the final stanza repeating the third line of the first stanza. Because of its pattern of repeated lines, the Pantoum works particularly well in conveying two perspectives, juxtapositions, arguments or push–pull kinds of motion. Christina's Pantoum juxtaposes protagonist Sally Little Song's sense of despair and hope. Though living as a slave with the sun beating on her back and hands raw from picking cotton, Sally dreams of freedom and continues to sing her song of hope. Christina's Pantoum effectively highlights the protagonist's indomitable spirit and love and value of family. In addition to writing the poem, having students write a paragraph of explanation requires them to be deliberate about the reasoning and critical thinking that informed their creative writing choices. An example explanation accompanies Christina's Pantoum.

While many of the stories referenced in this chapter are difficult to read because of the sometimes devastating circumstances the female protagonists have to endure, they paint a picture of purpose, determination, and perseverance to which girls might aspire. Through personal sacrifice and a willingness to confront injustices that arise as a result of various forms of religious, political, and cultural patriarchy, war, oppression, and loss, the protagonists of these novels contribute to the empowerment of the girls who read them. Additionally, the teaching strategies serve as reminders that when we encourage independent expression, we enable all readers to think broadly, freely, and creatively and to respond in ways that not only result in interesting displays of learning, but also work to ensure that the learning is personalized and relevant and, therefore, much more likely to last in meaningful ways.

Works Cited

Al-Windawi, Thura. *Thura's Diary: My Life in Wartime Iraq*. New York: Viking, 2004. Print.

Badoe, Adwoa. *Between Sisters*. Toronto: Groundwood, 2010. Print.

DeFelice, Cynthia. *Nowhere to Call Home*. New York: Harper Trophy, 1999. Print.

Elliott, L.M. *Annie, Between the States*. New York: Katherine Tegen, 2004. Print.

Engberg, Gillian. "In the Name of God." *Booklist*, 15 April 2007: 38. Print.

Frank, Anne. *The Diary of a Young Girl: The Definitive Edition*. Eds. Otto H. Frank and Mirjam Pressler. New York: Doubleday, 2005. Print.

Garland, Sherry. *Song of the Buffalo Boy*. San Diego, CA: Harcourt Brace, 1992. Print.

Hillman, Laura. *I Will Plant You a Lilac Tree: A Memoir of a Schindler's List Survivor*. New York: Atheneum, 2005. Print.

Houston, Jeanne Wakatsuki and James D. Houston. *Farewell to Manzanar*. New York: Bantam, 1973. Print.

Jiang, Ji Li. *Red Scarf Girl: A Memoir of the Cultural Revolution*. New York: Harper Collins, 1997. Print.

Jolin, Paula. *In the Name of God*. New York: Square Fish, 2007. Print.

Kamara, Mariatu with Susan McClelland. *The Bite of the Mango*. Toronto: Annick, 2008. Print.

Krisher, Trudy. *Fallout*. New York: Holiday House, 2006. Print.

——*Spite Fences*. New York: Bantam, 1994. Print.

——*Uncommon Faith*. New York: Holiday House, 2003. Print.

Li, Moying. *Snow Falling in Spring*. New York: Farrar, Straus and Giroux, 2008. Print.

Lowry, Lois. *Number the Stars*. New York: Yearling, 1989. Print.

McCormick, Patricia. *Sold*. New York: Hyperion, 2006. Print.

Park, Linda Sue. *A Long Walk to Water*. New York: Clarion, 2010. Print.

——*When My Name Was Keoko*. New York: Dell Yearling, 2002. Print.

Reit, Seymour. *Behind Rebel Lines: The Incredible Story of Emma Edmonds, Civil War Spy*. San Diego, CA: Gulliver, 1998. Print.

Rinaldi, Ann. *Hang a Thousand Trees with Ribbons: The Story of Phillis Wheatley*. New York: Scholastic, 1996. Print.

Schmidt, Gary D. *Lizzie Bright and the Buckminster Boy*. New York: Clarion, 2004. Print.

Stratton, Allan. *Chanda's Secrets*. Toronto: Annick, 2004. Print.

Venkatraman, Padma. *Climbing the Stairs*. New York: Putnam, 2008. Print.

Whelan, Gloria. *Angel on the Square*. New York: Scholastic, 2001. Print.

——*Homeless Bird*. New York: Harper Trophy, 2000. Print.

Wilson, Diane Lee. *Firehorse*. New York: Simon and Schuster, 2006. Print.

Woods, Brenda. *My Name Is Sally Little Song*. New York: G.P. Putman's Sons, 2006. Print.

Yu, Chun. *Little Green*. New York: Simon and Schuster, 2005. Print.

Zusak, Markus. *The Book Thief*. New York: Knopf, 2005. Print.

3

EMPOWERMENT, YA IMMIGRANT LITERATURE, AND GIRLS

Rosemary Horowitz and Joanne Brown

In the last two decades, YAL has increasingly embraced narratives about adolescents immigrating to the United States. The stories of young people leaving their native lands and adjusting to a new country—with all the complexities that such changes involve—have proven compelling to young American readers, girls perhaps in particular. In her seminal text on American female adolescents, Mary Pipher uses the metaphor "a new land" to analyze the changes in young girls that leave their parents baffled, and the girls themselves susceptible to all kinds of pressures. Pipher is referring, of course, to a figurative new land, but the challenges of adolescence are heightened when the new land is a literal one.

It can be argued that immigration to this country began when people crossed the existing land bridge between Siberia and Alaska. One could also argue that immigration began with the pilgrims who crossed the Atlantic to arrive at Plymouth Rock, or perhaps with the settlers who established Jamestown.[1] However, in his introduction to *Immigrant Voices*, Gordon Hutner argues that the initial newcomers to what would become the United States were more emigrants than immigrants. As Hutner defines the difference, the former are "best understood by where they are coming from," motivated by a desire to depart their native lands rather than by a wish to settle in a specific country. In contrast, Hutner says that immigrants are "more fully characterized by where it is they are going. … Most [early newcomers] to America came out of [a] desire to leave home, not out of a desire, specifically, to be in America," and "perhaps only when America could offer the benefits of being the United States does it make more useful cultural sense" to speak of immigration (x).

This distinction is useful in identifying the beginning of immigration to the United States. In Hutner's definition, it began with the notion that people could agree to govern themselves under laws established for the common good, a belief that decisively established itself in the nineteenth century when the young

American states achieved a firm identity as the United States. It is important to note that Hutner excludes Africans who were brought to America as slaves. According to Louis Mendoza and S. Shankar in their introduction to *Crossing into America: The New Literature of Immigration,* mass immigration to America began more than half a century after the nation's founding, more specifically in the 1840s when immigrants set off for "a new life in a new country with new laws," these immigrants being "individuals with varying degrees of ability to choose to make the journey" (xvi).

The momentous decision to emigrate severs the travelers from their traditional, accustomed worlds and transplants them in a strange new world, strangers among strangers with strange customs. Given the difficulties of immigration, what would prompt people to pull up roots and cross a treacherous ocean to an uncertain destination? Their stories are stories of ordinary people made extraordinary by undertaking an extraordinary experience. Although the immigrants came in waves of groups with shared ethnicity, for example, the Irish, the Italians, the Jews of Eastern Europe, these groups consisted of individuals with distinct motives and coping skills. Roger Daniels puts the complexity clearly: "[W]e must remember that migration is carried on by individual immigrants who, although their actions may conform to larger patterns, are each acting on what, to them, is a unique combination of motives" (22).

Daniels relies upon "a few special words to facilitate description of some of the major factors in migration" (17). The chief factors are *push, pull,* and *means.* This push–pull theory has become a classic explanation of immigration theory, which has been discussed in works by scholars such as Ronald Takaki, L. Edward Purcell, Thomas Dublin, as well as Carola Suarez-Orozco and Marcelo M. Suarez-Orozco. Specifically, *push* refers to those circumstances in the immigrants' native land that encourage or necessitate immigration, such as politics and economics. *Pull* refers to those attractive features in the migrants' destination, such as improved standard of living, promises of political or religious freedom, and climate—or, as Ronald Takaki defines it, "America's demand for labor as well as … their own dreams for a better life" (12). Although these terms seem to imply that immigrants are objects, acted upon rather than acting from their own sense of agency, in deciding to emigrate they control to some degree the shape of their voyage, for example, where, when, and how, and the various outcomes, dependent to a large degree upon the immigrants themselves.

Daniels maintains that most *push* and *pull* forces are, in the final analysis, economic, which means that the *push* and *pull* categories are not mutually exclusive. He contrasts the life in Europe that the immigrants have chosen to leave behind—structures that ensured ongoing, inherited poverty with little or no chance of upward mobility, and oppression that affected, to single out the most egregious examples, the Irish, Eastern European Jews, the Armenians, and the Poles—with the freedom and prosperity promised by the land across the sea.

The third term, *means,* is less often cited in analyzing immigrant histories than *push* and *pull,* but it, too, may yield valuable insights. Daniels defines it as "shorthand for the ability to migrate": affordable transportation, minor or no restraints on leaving the country of origin, and "the absence of effective barriers at the destination" (17). All of these terms are useful in considering perspectives in immigration literature for young adults.

Journeys as quests have long provided literary plot structures whose central conflicts involve a search for self-identity, a common theme in YAL. Certainly, such literature about immigrants and immigration portrays its young characters in some depth and allows readers to understand not only the motives that prompted those individuals to leave their native lands but also, often, the emotional ambivalence resulting from this rupture with an established way of life. Immigration narratives inevitably put special emphasis on this theme as the characters struggle to determine who they are as they adjust to new cultures and social expectations. Furthermore, YAL often strives to be optimistic, and YA tales of immigration are similar in that they almost always lead to increased maturity and self-awareness. The work of Robert Cormier is one important exception.

Keeping in mind the basic considerations of immigration, this chapter examines four novels that detail the situations that prompted girls and their families to leave their native lands and discusses how the girls coped with the departures, the difficulties of the journey to the United States, and the adjustment to life in the new country. It traces in two pairs of novels the development of the heroines as they grow increasingly empowered by their situations rather than disabled by them. The first set of novels comprises *Nory Ryan's Song* and its sequel *Maggie's Door* by Patricia Reilly Giff. This is the story of twelve-year-old Nory Ryan and her childhood years in the Irish village of Maiden Bay and her journey to America in the mid-1880s. The potato famine and the resultant starvation in Ireland *push* the Ryan family's move to America. The second set is *Double Crossing* and its sequel *Cursing Columbus* by Eve Tal. The books tell the story of Binyumin Balaban and his eleven-year-old daughter Raizel on their journey from Russia to America at the turn of the twentieth century and their eventual reunion with the rest of their immigrant family in New York. The members of the Balaban family leave their country as a result of the pogroms against the Jews; thus their immigrant story is also one of *push*. The development of the heroine in the immigration story may be seen as a through line by which American adolescent girls may reflect on their own circumstances as they embark on personal journeys to womanhood.

The concept of empowerment is central to understanding the heroines of these two novel sets. Although there are many theories of empowerment, this chapter relies on the work of the psychologists Lauren Benet Cattaneo and Aliya R. Chapman, who have developed a comprehensive model that has a great deal of explanatory value. Cattaneo and Chapman define empowerment as:

> an iterative process by which a person who lacks power sets a personally meaningful goal toward increasing power, takes action toward that goal, and observes and reflects on the impact of this action, drawing on his or her evolving self-efficacy, knowledge and competence related to the goal. (647)

Of the three aspects of empowerment listed, Cattaneo and Chapman consider self-efficacy to be the central one. A working definition of self-efficacy is the belief in one's abilities to achieve one's goals. The goal may be in service of the individual or the collective. In either case, achieving goals requires action. With regard to the heroines in the novels discussed, the types of actions the girls exhibit include acting purposefully, thinking independently, exhibiting confidence, countering role expectations, questioning conventional wisdom, and taking charge. To Cattaneo and Chapman, the empowerment process is a dynamic one. Regarding the two protagonists Nory and Raizel, this means that sometimes they are proactive and sometimes they are reactive. Cattaneo and Chapman further define empowerment as an iterative action-reflective process, which is a process in which one acts and then considers one's actions, and then acts again. This action–reflection relationship appears in all of the novels considered.

Acting Purposefully

To act purposefully means attempting to influence circumstances and not letting events determine one's fate or the fate of others. The belief that one may have an effect on others is an important aspect of agency. In all of the stories, the two heroines, Nory and Raizel, take decisive action at different times in the novels in order to benefit either themselves or the people around them. Although at times the girls are fearful or wish that someone else could take over and make the decision, they, nevertheless, act when necessary. In many instances during the novels, Nory's and Raizel's actions affect their own life and their family's.

In *Nory Ryan's Song*, when Devlin, the landlord's rent collector, appears at the Ryan's home to demand that the family deliver its cow and pig to the docks, Nory's grandfather vows to walk to Galway in search of her father. Nory insists that her sister Celia accompany the grandfather, knowing that staying alone in the house with their younger brother Patch would be beyond Celia's capabilities. By contrast, Nory feels secure in her own abilities to care for Patch. Her sense of responsibility to Patch is quite clear. Later on, Nory's friend Sean tells her that his brothers earned money on the docks at Galway before they sailed for America and that they left him a ticket for one more person. Nory is offered the ticket as their friend. She refuses the offer and sends Patch instead. Here again, she trusts in her own ability to survive. As it turns out, Nory overtakes Patch and his travel companions later in the novel en route to the ship with another ticket she was offered.

At another point in the story, Nory decides that she must find food for her family. She asks Sean to help her, resulting in this exchange:

> "I am going out to the cliffs … Like Tague. I'll take the eggs of the wild birds if I can find them."
>
> "You can't go down on a rope," he said. "Tague was killed that way. You know that."

"Do you think I'm going to die for want of food," I asked, "when it's there on the cliffs waiting for me?" But even as I said it I wondered if I could do it. (121)

Nory decides to go to the cliff, even though she is aware of the danger. In spite of her resolve, she still wonders if she is able to climb the rocks. However, she will try any method of obtaining food. To her, acting is better than simply waiting. Nory's deliberate action continues in *Maggie's Door*. For example, after she cuts herself on a rock, she forces herself to remember what she learned from Anna, the village healer, about how to stop bleeding. She remembers that Anna taught her to use a spider web to cover a wound. With that, Nory finds a web to wrap around her foot. Instead of panicking, Nory musters her memory of Anna for inspiration. Although from time to time she doubts her healing ability, Nory does in fact cure Erika, a passenger on the ship who is apparently suffering from hepatitis, and Sean, who is burned on the stove in the ship's kitchen.

Raizel, in *Double Crossing*, also acts with purpose. During a scene where the group of travelers is going through a river, Raizel grabs Soyrele, a fellow traveler, when the young girl falls into the water. The author describes Raizel's actions during that episode:

"Papa!"
Soyrele shrieked as she lost her grip on Yakov's neck and fell backwards into the water.
I threw myself forward and pushed her back up as my feet flew out from under me. (90)

In this scene, Raizel saves Soyrele from drowning, but then she loses her own balance and has to be rescued herself. Here again, as when Nory determines she will brave the cliffs for food, a girl does not have to be perfect, but she has to do something when possible. By the end of the novel, Raizel is even able to help her father. At a session with an immigration officer at their second crossing, Raizel steps in as the officer begins his questioning of her father. When he calls for a translator, she tells the officer: "'I speak a little English.' The words flew out of my mouth like a frightened bird. My stomach turned over with fear. I looked at Papa. He nodded and gave me a tight smile" (255). Raizel does not want to risk another rejection at Ellis Island, so despite her fear she makes up a story that she hopes will convince the officer to grant them permission to enter the country. Her answers satisfy the officer, and he approves their entry application. Afterwards, Raizel's father compliments her by saying "What a smart daughter I have!" (258). Thus, by the end of their journey, Raizel is able to act as a spokesperson for her father. She continues her development in *Cursing Columbus*, gaining knowledge and agency in her thoughts and deeds.

Nory and Raizel teach contemporary readers that whether she wields power on behalf of personal, family, or community goals, the empowered girl takes responsibility for her actions. She mobilizes her resources to achieve her self-defined goals and, despite obstacles, keeps going, keeps growing, and keeps believing in her own abilities.

Thinking Independently

The ability to think independently is another critical aspect of agency. Empowered girls deal with life choices either by themselves or in consultation with others when necessary. They gain mastery and confidence with each success. Failure teaches them about the value of resilience and sustained effort and does not stop them. As autonomous girls, Nory and Raizel make what are often difficult decisions based on self-defined goals.

In *Nory Ryan's Song*, Nory decides to sell her shawl to buy food. The author describes Nory's thoughts: "I kept walking, planning. How much would I get for the shawl? Whom shall I sell it to? What was the most important thing to buy afterward?" (110). Since there are no adults who will answer these questions, Nory has to decide the best course of action for herself and her family. Even though she does have a major setback when her packages are stolen, she does not give up on the main objective of finding food. In *Maggie's Door*, Nory continues to rely on her independent thinking. When she overtakes Mrs. Mallon, Sean's mother, and Patch on their way to the ship, Nory hopes that Mrs. Mallon will share some of the burden of the trip. However, Nory quickly sees Mrs. Mallon's despair. Even though Nory begs Mrs. Mallon to stay, the woman decides to return home. Gaining strength by thinking of her own grandfather and Anna, Nory informs Patch that she will take him to the ship and to their family.

Raizel, in *Double Crossing*, faces very important choices of her own. At one point, Mrs. Goldenberg, another traveler on the same ship, offers Raizel the opportunity to stay in Antwerp after Raizel and her father were returned to Europe after having been denied permission to enter America. However, Mrs. Goldenberg does not extend the offer to Raizel's father. After thinking about her options, Raizel tells Mrs. Goldenberg:

> "I decided to return with Papa."
> Mrs. Goldenberg sighed. "I expected as much. Your papa must have been opposed to the idea."
> "I didn't tell him."
> Mrs. Goldenberg cocked her head. "Such an important decision and you didn't consult your papa?"
> "It was my decision to make, not Papa's. I thank you for offering me the chance." (238)

By rejecting Mrs. Goldenberg's offer to stay in a place that offers her so much, Raizel knows that she is giving up school, fancy clothes, fine food, concerts, vacations, and other luxuries. However, she decides on her own to put her family above riches. She knows her priorities and acts on them. Raizel is true to herself and her deepest values, even though it might mean sacrificing the education she longs to have. Once in America though, Raizel holds fast to her dreams and continues to strive to achieve her goals in spite of a number of obstacles faced by her in the sequel *Cursing Columbus*.

Taken together, these four novels suggest that immigrant girls, like their modern adolescent readers, share common goals. They want the best thing for themselves, their families, and those they love. In addition, the protagonists and their readers must often rely on the same inner strength needed to negotiate the path from girlhood to womanhood.

Countering Expectations

Parents, teachers, friends, relatives, and various other people in girls' lives have their own beliefs about the proper behavior for girls. However, the empowered girl does not automatically accept the assigned roles and expectations. Rather, she considers the consequences of the ideas and ideals of others, along with her own goals. She believes that her dreams count. As girls who are in the process of becoming empowered, Raizel and Nory consider the effect of gender and numerous other restrictions on their lives.

In *Nory Ryan's Song*, when she is desperate for food, Nory asks the Mallon brothers if she may go fishing with them in their currach boat:

> "I won't take up that much room," I told them. "I'll sit on the bottom, between the seats. All I need is a line and a hook." …
>   "There's no room, Nory, and you don't know how to fish beyond the surf."
> "Please," I said. "Please."
> I could hear Liam, too. "Ah, Nory," he was saying, "ah."
> Was he feeling sorry for me?
>   Suddenly I was angry. Angrier than I could ever remember. I picked up a stone and threw it as hard as I could. It bounced off the currach with a small thud. (64–65)

The brothers know that Nory is as hungry as they are, but they still do not give her the chance to fish. Instead, they tell her to wait for Sean and to pick up seafood on the shore with him. This is absolutely the wrong advice for Nory, who hates to wait. She is not willing to limit herself to others' definitions of what girls can do.

Raizel, in *Double Crossing*, is also not content to limit herself. She constantly wishes that she could read and study. Since in her culture only boys attend school, she sometimes wishes she were a boy. She envies her older brother, Lemmel, because he is expected to attend school, even though he is not interested in education. Raizel is clear in her desire and regularly expresses her wishes. When talking to Lemmel, she notes:

> "It's not fair," I said. "You go to school and hate it. I can't go to school and love it. If only Jibatov had a school for girls, or I could take lessons from a private tutor like Leah does. I would love to read the stories about David and Goliath, Ruth and Esther."
>
> "We never read stories. All we read are prayers. It's boring."
>
> "Still you can read them if you want to. And you can read Sholem Aleichem and … " (25)

Raizel knows that excluding the girls from education is not right. She wants to read the biblical stories, such as those of David and Goliath, as well as secular stories, such as those of Sholem Aleichem. Although her father understands Raizel's desire, in his worldview girls do not need to read and write. She knows her father expects her to be a good wife and mother, but wonders why she cannot do that and be literate. When she finds out that in America girls go to school, Raizel no longer wishes to be a boy. In America, it is possible to be herself and be educated. Ironically, in *Cursing Columbus* Raizel has to stand up against not her father's views about girls but her mother's. When her mother reminds Raizel to pick up her younger brother after school so that they can go shopping, Raizel asks her mother for permission to go to the library. Her mother says: "Always with her head in a book, that one. You went last week and we need food" (21). Helping her mother in the house interferes with Raizel's trips to the library and her school work, and she grows resentful.

In life and in literature, girls have to decide to accept or to challenge the status quo, no matter what the context. In either case, the empowered girl must sometimes act on behalf of her self-defined goals for her own good. Sometimes she strives for autonomy from a group; other times she strives for solidarity with the group. Just like their fictional counterparts, contemporary female readers understand these difficult choices and strive to act accordingly.

Exhibiting Confidence

Girls need to believe in themselves in order to take an active role in their lives. Confidence in one's self, resistance to peer pressure, a focus on one's goals, and feelings of security are some of the inner resources needed to achieve goals. In these novels, Raizel and Nory show how much a girl may accomplish when her confidence is not diminished.

There is a scene in *Nory Ryan's Song* where Nory bargains with Devlin, the rent collector, for some food in exchange for the medicine that Devlin wants for the landlord. She starts by saying:

> "Anna is not healing now. … She needs her dog."
>
> Devlin looked back and up at the landlord's house. "I will send the dog."

> I closed my eyes. "Food."
>
> "There is little food in the whole land."
>
> "It has gone to England," I said bitterly. "But someday the potatoes will grow again. She will need seed potatoes and help planting them."
>
> "All right."
>
> "I will ask her." I stopped and started again. "As soon as she has the dog and food. Just a little food. She doesn't need much."
>
> "Don't go too far," he said, but nodded just the slightest bit. (138)

With this vague threat, Devlin indicates that the bargaining is over. Nory is clearly nervous in this encounter with Devlin, as indicated by her hesitation before her final demand. She will not ask Anna for the cure that Devlin requests until she is assured that Anna has her food and will get back her dog, which has been taken by the landlord as punishment. Even though Nory is vulnerable, Devlin agrees for the sake of obtaining the cure. She leverages what she can to get Anna what she needs. Bargaining with Devlin is not a small matter for Nory, as he has the means to take everything away from the families; but Nory stands up to him and in the end wrests what she needs from him.

When Raizel's father in *Double Crossing* announces to his family that he has two tickets for America, Raizel reluctantly raises the possibility that she might accompany him. Her brother Lemmel laughs at her, saying "Nobody would let a girl go to America" (25). Later that night, considering this insult to girls, Raizel thinks to herself: "What if I were a girl? Girls were important too. Girls had babies and kept home and cooked the meals. So why did men think they were more important?" (26). At this point in the novel, Raizel focuses on traditional female roles, while also claiming their importance. Later in the novel Raizel's desire for education motivates her to request her father's permission to go to school. She gathers herself to speak:

> I took a deep breath for courage. "Papa, sometimes I do feel like a dry well. There are so many things I want to know." I force myself to look Papa straight in the eyes. "May I go to school in America, Papa? That is, if there is a school near where we live. I will clean the house and cook for you after school. I promise, Papa." (109)

With the assertive gesture of looking into her father's eyes, Raizel forces him to make direct eye contact with her too. Although he turns her down then by undermining her desire, she reiterates her request numerous times through the novel. She will not be deterred, and her actions show that perseverance is a necessary trait in the process of empowerment.

Later, in *Cursing Columbus*, her father grows to understand how much education may help one become successful. Unlike her brother Lemmel, who has difficulty adjusting to the new country and begins a life of petty crime, even stealing from his parents, Raizel knows what she wants and what she can accomplish. Her sense of self, coupled with her personal values, give her the means to deal with life in America, including the challenges of her home, neighborhood, family beliefs, school, and other situations.

The lives of Nory and Raizel show that empowered girls draw on their knowledge and competency to fulfill goals. In turn, that increases their confidence and their willingness to take further action. YA female readers may use the lessons taught by the two heroines to prepare themselves to face their own challenges. Though circumstances may differ, the means required for satisfactory resolution are often the same.

Questioning Conventional Wisdom

During their upbringing, girls learn the norms and values of their culture, along with a multitude of other lessons. However, occasions arise when an evaluation of those norms and values becomes necessary. Not surprisingly, given their penchant for agency, Nory and Raizel both evaluate the rules that govern their lives. While the ability to effect changes depends on the nature of the rules, nonetheless Nory and Raizel are willing to look at and evaluate the restrictions.

Nory Ryan's Song condemns the callousness of the British who confiscate large tracts of land from the native Irish Catholics and then rent that land to their own poor Irish tenants. Nory expresses her disdain for the system that impoverishes her and her family, along with so many of her compatriots. At one point, her brother Patch asks if he will be given some milk. Nory replies: "No. The cow is gone. Gone with Muc and Biddy to England. They will be English animals now, not Irish" (104). Nory is referring to the fact that the English took her family's cow, pigs, and chickens and left nothing for the family. The way in which the animals change their nationality in her description shows her underlying criticism of the English and their behavior.

While Nory reflects on politics, Raizel reflects on religion. At one point in *Double Crossing*, Raizel asks her father to give up some of his traditional religious beliefs in order to possibly ease their way into America. She has violated some of the commandments and suggests that he do the same. She presses him about Judaism: "Papa, if you shave your beard, change your clothes and eat unkosher food, will you still be Jewish?" (205). By way of an answer, he tells her that men, but not women, are required to obey the commandants of the Jewish tradition. She then reflects on what it means to be a Jew and wonders: "Did your outside matter if your inside was still the same"? (206). In this way, Raizel is clearly seen grappling with obedience to the laws of Judaism, the most fundamental tenet of her religion.

In *Cursing Columbus*, Raizel begins to question her mother's cultural views regarding the life of a girl. In the traditional life in the Ukraine, girls worked at home until they married. Everything was arranged, and girls had no say in anything, even in the choosing of their own husbands. Raizel knows that she wants more from life than working in a factory before marriage and then cooking, cleaning, and raising children afterwards with a man she might not even love. She imagines going to college and studying to be a teacher, but she cannot hope to achieve that goal unless she convinces her mother that school is important. Given that her mother makes all the decisions in their home, Raizel knows that changing her mother's mind will be very hard. Ironically, after coming to America Raizel's father grows to understand that education is the way to success for both boys and girls.

As is clear, Nory and Raizel are willing to examine their world and challenge its restrictions. Whether it is politics, religion, education, or some other societal or cultural structure, young adult female readers will be well served to reflect on the restrictions of their own lives and take action to the best of their ability within the context of their lives to make changes. Though this will not always be easy, it is necessary if girls are to enact the wisdom they gain from their own observations of the world.

Taking Charge

Leadership may be defined as the ability to influence the behavior of others. Within that definition, it is recognized that there are different types of leaders. Additionally, different situations call for different leadership styles. Some people eagerly assume responsibility, while others may be asked to do so. Some leaders act on a grand scale. For others, the scope is more limited. In the four novels under discussion, Nory leads with her ability to sing and to heal, while Raizel leads with her ability to tell stories. The girls' strengths are different but are directed toward a similar end.

Maggie, the older sister, tells Nory in *Nory Ryan's Song* that the family appreciates her singing: "'You are the heart of this family,' she said, 'with your songs'" (26). The family looks to Nory and her songs for comfort on numerous occasions. She also knows how to use plants to heal people. In *Maggie's Door*, Nory continues to assume responsibility. For instance, at one point while on the ship, she insists she needs to boil water for the flowers to cure Eliza's hepatitis. About that Giff writes:

> She went toward the stairs, but there was a ragged line in front of her. "Please," she said, trying to push through. Someone pushed back, but she had her foot on the step and managed to climb, pushing away the hand that reached out to grab her sleeve. (97)

When Garvey, one of the crew members, hears the determination in Nory's voice, he tells the crowd to leave her alone. In deference to her insistence, he calls her "your honor." Even if he is teasing, Nory will not be deterred from her task. Later Garvey's amusement turns to admiration as he watches her push her way past stronger people in order to boil the water.

In *Double Crossing*, Raizel's leadership stems from her storytelling ability. Even before she sets out with her father on their journey to America, her storytelling talents are evident in her dealings with her sisters and brothers. Then later on during the trip, when other children she meets are scared, Raizel comforts them with her tales. During one scene in the novel, after listening to one of her stories, Mrs. Goldenberg says: "That's marvelous, Raizel. You have a gift for making words come alive" (189). By recognizing Raizel's talent, Mrs. Goldenberg encourages Raizel to continue mastering her abilities. Through the course of the novel, Raizel uses those abilities to tell stories to calm children, comfort adults, entertain family members, still her own fears, and for other purposes. She does so at home, on the trip across the border, on the ship, and elsewhere. Sometimes people look to her and her storytelling talents to solve problems. Other times she takes the initiative on her own to improve the situation.

Storytelling is Raizel's way of affecting the people around her and changing their behavior, whereas singing and healing are Nory's. By their singing, healing, and storytelling abilities, Nory and Raizel each exhibit leadership. Their style is not necessarily a boy's style or even a common one, but the point made is that a girl may have and use her abilities in a variety of traditional or nontraditional settings. It is her ability to exert control over a situation, to whatever extent possible, that marks a girl as an active participant in her own life.

Conclusion

Narratives of immigration with heroines add much to both the school curriculum and the personal growth of students. The immigrant girls in these stories and others like them may function as role models for YA female readers because the girls who leave their homes for unfamiliar places face many challenges. Differences in language, customs, responsibilities, food, dress, manners, religion, race, sexuality, identity, class, and other matters confront them. Contemporary girls learn that empowerment is a process that entails negotiating challenges, taking risks, and keeping focused on goals. These behaviors are relevant to all girls, while boys too may learn from them. Thus, in the lives of immigrant girl protagonists, all young readers may find parallels to their own.

Note

1 The definition of "immigrants" and their motives for leaving their native lands is adapted from *Immigration Narratives in Young Adult Literature* by Joanne Brown (Lanham, MD: Scarecrow Press, 2010).

Works Cited

Cattaneo, Lauren Benet and Aliya R. Chapman. "The Process of Empowerment: A Model for Use in Research and Practice." *American Psychologist* 65.7 (October 2010): 646–59. Web.

Daniels, Roger. *Coming to America: A History of Immigration and Ethnicity in American Life.* New York: Perennial, 2002. Print.

Dublin, Thomas, ed. *Immigrant Voices.* Urbana, IL: University of Illinois Press, 1993. Print.

Giff, Patricia Reilly. *Nory Ryan's Song.* New York: Yearling, 2000. Print.

——*Maggie's Door.* New York: Wendy Lamb Books, 2003. Print.

Hutner, Gordon, ed. *Immigrant Voices: Twenty-Four Narratives on Becoming an American.* New York: Signet Classic, 1999. Print.

Mendoza, Louis, and S. Shankar. *Crossing into America: The New Literature of Immigration.* New York: The New Press, 2003. Print.

Pipher, Mary. *Reviving Ophelia: Saving the Selves to Adolescent Girls.* New York: Ballantine, 1994. Print.

Purcell, L. Edward. *Immigration.* Phoenix, AZ: Oryx, 1995. Print.

Suarez-Orozco, Carola, and Marcelo M. Suarez-Orozco. *Children of Immigrants.* Cambridge, MA: Harvard University Press, 2002. Print.

Takaki, Ronald. *A Different Mirror: A History of Multicultural America.* New York: Little & Brown, 1993. Print.

Tal, Eve. *Double Crossing.* El Paso, TX: Cinco Puntos Press, 2005. Print.

——*Cursing Columbus.* El Paso, TX: Cinco Puntos Press, 2009. Print.

4

THROUGH A LESBIAN LENS

Girls, Femininity, and Sexuality on a Reading Spectrum

Beth Younger

When I was a young girl reading *Harriet the Spy*, I instinctively knew that there was something about Harriet that made adults nervous. I knew that I too often made adults nervous. What I did not know then was that Harriet stood as a symbol of pre-sexual lesbian identity. Young Harriet is a representation with whom many young women, lesbian and heterosexual, identify because her character is not stereotypically feminine. Harriet is a gender-bending, smart, capable, and sensitive young pre-teen who challenges the adult world with her idiosyncratic behavior and comportment. In many ways, Harriet is (and has been) a queer icon, an icon of resistance to hetero-normative culture. But Harriet is not the only literary figure in children's or Young Adult literature (YAL) who challenges cultural ideals of femininity and sexuality; in the early twenty-first century we are progressively finding more and more fictions in our libraries and classrooms with characters who complicate ideas of what it means to be female, young, and gendered in contemporary culture. No longer are the issues that arise for these characters secondary to the conflicts of their more traditional counterparts. Their nonconforming gender choices are relevant and even critical for understanding the complexities of the world in which we live.

When girls read books about fictional young women, they may hope to identify with the protagonist. They may also begin to define themselves by rejecting or resisting the depictions they read as they seek to come to terms with their own identities in a culture that continues to marginalize girls, especially girls who do not conform to ideal standards of acceptable femininity or beauty. We know that girls and young women struggle with body image and with appearance; these kinds of issues have been pervasive in Western culture for decades. And while YAL in general has made room for all different kinds of girls with a vast array of beauties, sexualities, strengths, and personalities, including girls who vividly resist many of the stereotypical standards, it is in subsets of YAL fiction like LGBTQ that we find the greatest challenge to long-held cultural norms. Contemporary YAL that introduces relatable lesbian characters and strong girl characters has created a very special and almost liminal space where young women can read about their peers and themselves and re-imagine (and perhaps re-define) what it means to be female in the twenty-first century. In the ever-increasing array of novels now available, the LGBTQ subset has a progressive history of interaction with cultural norms and ideals. While it is worth noting that YA books about gay males outnumber books about gay females, perhaps suggesting yet another way girls and their developing sexual desires are marginalized, there still exists a range of complex and intriguing texts that depict young women in formation in terms of sexual orientation, identity, and femininity. Many of these texts depict much more than simply a coming of age or identity formation narrative focused on sexual orientation; they also grapple with issues of appearance, notions of femininity, and gender fluidity.

In this chapter I propose a way for all girls—lesbian, questioning, bisexual, or heterosexual—to read novels and stories that include various representations of femininity and femaleness, in order to help them to identify for themselves and each other where they might fit along the spectrum of femininity. I see the spectrum of femininity as an ideological tool that includes all sexual orientations while making significant room for lesbianism since female homosexuality still exists mostly outside the dominant culture. This reading space (or practice) focuses on how novels about girls and young women trying to stay true to their evolving selves allow for the depiction of character development along a spectrum. One way to introduce all students to the idea of the spectrum is to use a rainbow, a symbol of solidarity with the gay and lesbian community that can easily be constructed to focus on issues of justice or equality and how those issues impact gender construction and sexuality. The point here is not to supply a predetermined spectrum, but to help students think about how to meaningfully and purposefully construct a model of discovery that serves as a bridge for varying perspectives. Adult guidance is useful, but an important part of the learning process is that readers are involved in constructing their own spectrum in order that they may thoughtfully consider choices along the way. Beginning with the rainbow allows students to think about what a spectrum means through a symbol everyone knows and understands. A rainbow is also a part of nature, and in that sense the process of creating a spectrum of femininity through such an organizing principle acknowledges that while femininity may be seen by the dominant culture as having a "natural" trajectory, we also know there are many varieties of rainbows. Some are double. Some are seen only as a patch of color in the sky. Most importantly, throughout history the rainbow has meant different things to different people. By superimposing various understandings of femininity on the basic spectrum, a questioning of the cultural norm of what constitutes "natural" can occur.

As we know, sexuality and gender identity are not inextricably linked. As Queer Theory reminds us, reading through this lens allows scholars and educators to visualize and put into practice a way to read against the constant bombardment of hetero-normativity and stereotypical forms of femininity that girls encounter each and every day. Queer Theory, then, according to William Turner, allows readers to view queerness not as a "synonym for homosexuality but as a descriptor of disruptions to prevailing cultural codes of sexual and gender normativity" (11). It is through this ideological lens that the chapter will provide a way for girls to read gender, femininity, and sexuality and thus learn to resist and reclaim what femininity and female mean to each one of them. What does it mean to be a "tomboy"? Can one be a lesbian and wear frilly dresses? If I like girls *and* boys, what does that make me? By posing and answering these and other questions about fictional characters, it is my hope that all girls will be able to reclaim gender identity and sexuality for themselves. Through the process of reading about disparate and varied female characters, lesbian, straight, and bisexual, they will be able to recognize that they have the power to (re)define what it means to be a girl.

Young women and girls know what is expected of them in terms of how they are "supposed" to be performing and grooming their gender identities—while they may not label it that way, they recognize the expectations. In what has become an important text, *Reviving Ophelia* by Mary Pipher documents myriad cases of young women struggling with body image because they do not believe they conform to the ideal standard of beauty. Pipher acknowledges "girls are terrified of being fat" (184); however, she also argues that: "Girls who stay connected to their true selves are also confused and sometimes overwhelmed. But they have made some commitment to understanding their lives. They think about their experiences. They do not give up on trying to resolve contradictions and make connections between events. … They will make many mistakes and misinterpret much of reality, but girls with true selves make a commitment to process and understand their experiences" (61).

Those concerned with a lack of reading materials that introduce a wide range of what constitutes femininity know that novel choice is important for opening up the conversation. Of course, the novels that may provoke the most reaction and controversy may not be available (or acceptable) for all classrooms, but I strongly suggest that, in order to push our students to critically think about the issues of justice, equality, and human rights that surround gender, we must expand our vision of what is "acceptable" in the middle school and high school classroom and bring as many challenging books as we can to the students. The National Council of Teachers of English (NCTE), Association for Middle Level Education (AMLE), and American Education Research Association (AERA) have all either made statements, partnered with GLBT organizations, or presented initiatives on the need for schools to more actively address issues of gender nonconformity. Even with that and young women in mind, I know that the novels I discuss in this chapter may not all make it into classrooms because making available YAL of any kind, especially stories with lesbian themes, is often still considered taboo. As Emily Meixner states in her 2009 *ALAN Review* article on LGBTQ in the classroom:

As we begin, then, to consider why this is, why LGBTQ literature continues to remain absent from most middle and high school classrooms, we focus our attention on two things. First, curriculum—specifically, the way in which the texts we privilege in class, either by explicitly teaching them or by giving them face time in an activity such as the book pass, become meaningful. We examine how it is that our curricular and methodological choices determine what educational theorist Michael Apple calls "the official knowledge" of our classrooms. (94)

In order to combat the kind of "official knowledge" referenced by Apple, such as privileging certain voices over others which often excludes voices of LGBTQ and other marginalized groups like girls, those who offer texts for reading choice must resist the urge to be safe and must also reject the monolithic voice of the dominant culture that would exclude some, if not all, YAL in the classroom.

When reading fiction, it is typical to discuss the qualities of characters and how their authors have created them to reflect certain traits and values. What if, when having these discussions, teachers simply asked readers to choose a protagonist and list her qualities? Such an entry to understanding character could be the beginning of the construction of a spectrum of femininity. Including books with lesbian or questioning protagonists for this process stimulates discussion because young female characters struggling with or even accepting a sexual orientation other than hetero are automatically coded by the dominant culture as being outside the appropriate boundaries of ideal femininity. These characters, then, have already been marked as other. They are not "regular." They are different. Such protagonists open the door to the larger conversation about what is and is not acceptable in terms of the dominant discourse on femininity and femaleness.

We know that adolescence is a time when many (if not most) teens feel "different." They feel awkward, uncomfortable, even weird. But it is important for educators to realize it is not for us to decide what "different" means for each reader. How do we know, after all? This is where novel choice becomes important. In the following sections of this chapter, I will first list and analyze several instances of YAL that introduce provocative female characters, some lesbian, some not. Each novel depicts a strong young woman who is dealing with some kind of difference. I will demonstrate how these female characters function to challenge traditional notions of femininity and hetero-normativity. In the last section, I will suggest some activities to facilitate classroom discussion and individual interaction with the aforementioned novels that coincide with my idea of considering a spectrum of femininity where all girls may be recognized.

One of the ways that young women discover what it means to be lesbian in a hetero-normative culture is through identification. By reading about and identifying with a lesbian character, a young woman may experience a shock or spark of recognition. As Sherrie Inness writes: "When lesbians read, they actively disassemble the dominant heterosexual plot, demonstrating that heterosexuality does not hold its culturally prescribed central role for all readers" (83). I also see this logic as applied to heterosexual readers in terms of femininity. Many girls do not fit the standard role of "girly" girl, and by reading against the grain, and for gender and sexuality, all girl readers, regardless of sexual orientation, can challenge the status quo. My goal is to inspire a reading and learning space and process that would include young girls in every stage of identity formation and of every sexual orientation. This process would encourage young women to read widely and to identify not only where each character—gay, straight, or otherwise—falls on the spectrum of femininity, but also what the space they occupy means in terms of acceptance and/or oppression. In each depiction discussed, I will illustrate how a spectrum of femininity can be used to help girls "read" and interpret fictional characters, themselves, and each other as unique and individual, in whatever spectrum space they may fall.

The Novels: From *Annie* to *Ash*

Nancy Garden's iconic *Annie on My Mind* (1982) is a lyrical narrative of two young women who fall in love. Their tale is framed by Liza's memory of their relationship and the obstacles the two encounter along the way. The story is fairly linear and mostly conventional; the young women face predictable resistance from their schools and families. But what makes the novel stand out is how romantic the narrative manages to be, and how deeply drawn the characters of Liza and Annie are. Both embody stereotypical feminine qualities (they are conventionally pretty, have long hair, and are slender), yet, significantly, when they venture outside the boundaries of their bodily comportment, they find themselves in serious trouble. An interesting and positive aspect of Garden's story is that Annie and Liza become increasingly comfortable with their sexualities as they begin to spend intimate time together. However, they also get "caught" messing around by a stuffy, uptight school administrator while house sitting. Further, Liza's "male" designated jacket also marks her as a lesbian. Later, at a bizarre "hearing" at the school, the administrator, Mrs. Poindexter, tries to articulate to Liza's mother what she finds so upsetting about Liza's attire:

> "Teenaged Girls," shouted Mrs. Poindexter, moving around to our side of the table and walking toward my mother, "do not usually try on lumber jackets. And I've never felt that your Liza had any particular interest in her hair. As a matter of fact, I have often felt that your daughter Eliza ... " (208)

As surreal as that scene now seems, the message is clear: Liza does not care about her appearance in a way that it is assumed a heterosexual girl would. She tries on a "lumber" jacket and does not care about her hair. It is laughable, but many young women (gay and straight) in my classes acknowledge that they currently fit into Mrs. Poindexter's description. The rules and regulations for what is marked as feminine may be more flexible in the twenty-first century, but certain accoutrements still mark a young woman as resistant to what is considered the ideal standard of femininity. For contemporary readers, Liza's resistance strikes a chord of recognition. In a pivotal scene even heterosexuality is skewered as dangerous. Early in the narrative Liza faces a dilemma when a few girls in her private school are running an ear-piercing business in the school's basement. Liza knows she is bound by the honor code to "tell," but she does not. Some of the piercings get infected—a graphic metaphor for the possible consequences of heterosexual intercourse. With this metaphor setting the tone for the rest of the novel, Liza and Annie's relationship takes shape outside the boundaries of heterosexual culture. Although it is not the most radical novel (Annie and Liza's romance mimics heterosexual patterns; they buy each other the same ring; they have romantic dinners), *Annie* sets the stage for future lesbian YA novels, depicting lesbian romance as having to overcome numerous obstacles and various forms of resistance, but, ultimately, enduring. Despite their adherence to traditional femininity, the forays Annie and Liza make into resisting the constraints of traditional femininity are worth noting and make for interesting and useful discussion as to where the girls might fit on a spectrum of femininity. Readers might place them closer to traditional femininity because of their prettiness, their hair, and even their expectations of what constitutes romantic behavior, but closer to gender neutral or masculine qualities because of Liza's resistance to makeup and personal grooming.

A more contemporary YA novel that approaches young lesbianism in a somewhat similar way is Sara Ryan's *Empress of the World* (2001). In many ways, it is a very standard romance novel—except it involves two girls instead of the usual heterosexual duo. The narrative takes place in a summer camp for gifted teens where Nicola (Nic) meets the unusually named Battle, whom she nicknames "beautiful hair girl." *Empress* is reminiscent of *Annie* in that the plot hinges on the resistance of one of the lovers to her own homosexuality; yet in *Empress* there is little or no resistance from the outside world—everyone in the story appears fine with two girls who fall in love, a commentary on the difference twenty years have made in social acceptance. However, on a personal level Battle still has trouble accepting that she could be in love with another girl, perhaps revealing why she is named thus. The plot almost becomes dysphoric, but is rescued by Battle's sudden change of heart. Battle allows herself to love Nic, and the two go off hand in hand. What is useful and intriguing about this narrative is how Battle, described as luminously beautiful by Nic, rejects traditional expectations of femininity by cutting off her incredible hair. During the hair-cutting scene, Battle explains that she is going to cut off all of her hair as a message to her parents. She reveals: "I wish only for them to see that I am not a doll to be dressed and played with" (77). While the message is to Battle's parents, for readers Battle's words serve as a very direct message about femininity and capitulation to social norms. Battle understands she has always been valued for her appearance. She also knows she cannot necessarily change the culture that has imposed that value, but she can change herself. Her shifting recognition of self makes Battle's space on a spectrum of femininity much more fluid. In fact, she might occupy two spaces: pre- and post-haircutting. Readers are able to consider her struggle and decide.

Kissing Kate (2003) by Lauren Myracle represents another kind of change altogether, as it depicts the long time friendship of Lissa and Kate, tested by their mutual attraction to each other. Lissa and Kate are two average teenage girls who stand just a little bit outside the boundaries of stereotypical femininity. Kate's mother has even asked them to dress more like "ladies." "You two have such darling figures," she chide[s]. "You need to accentuate them. Boys like to see a girl's curves" (14). One night at a party, the two inseparable friends end up kissing each other in a spontaneous moment of mutual intimacy. Now the two best friends must deal with a new aspect of their relationship. Kate rejects Lissa and begins dating a boy, which forces Lissa to come to terms with her own sexuality while losing her best friend. *Kate* challenges readers to consider what it means when someone you thought you knew changes into a person you barely know. In this novel of development, which really is not a romance story, Lissa learns as much about her evolving self as she does about what it means to be attracted to girls. Once she realizes Kate has turned from her and become even somewhat hostile after their shared kiss, she is forced to examine her emerging identity on her own.

One of the ways *Kate* marks feminine "otherness" is through Lissa's reluctance to befriend another young woman who strikes up a friendship with her. Lissa is wary of Ariel, who seems "different" and is truly unafraid to be herself. However, it is partially through this friendship with Ariel that Lissa learns to accept herself as she is—especially since Kate has rejected her and denied Lissa her sexuality by proclaiming: "I'm not like you, Lissa. I'm not a fucking dyke, all right?" (180). This moment of hatefulness shocks Lissa and, perhaps, readers, but it is a profound moment of recognition that Lissa's desires for Kate will not be reciprocated. Lissa is forced to move on, sad but wiser for the experience. Placing these two characters on a spectrum of femininity constitutes a challenge, since each occupies a liminal space. New questions arise, such as does behavior count when determining femininity or is appearance the most significant qualifier?

Julie Anne Peters' coming out narrative *Keeping You a Secret* (2003) is the story of Holland Jaeger. Holland is class president, a swimmer, an excellent student and all-around good girl who realizes she is a lesbian once she meets Cece, a new student in her high school. Holland's story follows what is a more standard coming out plot, but does so with good humor and thoughtful characterization. One of the lovely and most realistic qualities of the novel is how Holland slowly becomes aware of her sexual orientation—she has a boyfriend, but through her gradual interaction with Cece is slowly jolted into electric reality when the sparks of attraction fly. Out lesbians and gay men are often asked "how did you know you were gay?" or "when did you figure out you were a lesbian?" In *Keeping* the answer is revealed throughout the novel, and readers discover along with Holland the bigger picture of what her new attraction to Cece and her diminishing interest in her boyfriend means. The difference in affect is palpable, but the story becomes more than a coming out narrative. In the end, it is a novel of adolescent development set within the context of lesbian awakening.

Key to Holland's development is her awareness that her dislike of frilly attire and her love of babies are just attributes, qualities that many young women have. These qualities, readers must admit, are not indicative of any particular sexual orientation; they are just aspects of personality that many women possess. An important way that Peters constructs Holland's femininity is through her love of children; there is no doubt that she has a strong maternal instinct. Holland's character provides yet another stop along the spectrum of femininity, as she is a combination of stereo-typically approved feminine qualities alongside a few unusual qualities that can be read as more gender neutral. She defies the characterization of lesbians as not being maternal, giving pause again for questions about how the dominant discourse on what constitutes femininity has been determined.

Because it allows readers to enter a realm generally off limits for questions of femininity, Malinda Lo's retelling of the Cinderella story, *Ash* (2009), is a luminous and wondrous fantasy piece of YA fiction. Of all stories, fairy tales are the ones most ingrained with notions of girlhood desires. Subtitled "It's not the fairy tale you remember," *Ash* re-imagines what it might be like if Cinderella fell in love with another young woman. As a character, Ash takes a bigger step along the spectrum of femininity than does Annie, Lissa, or Holland. This fantasy novel truly challenges gender stereotypes, as Ash makes her way through her father's death and subsequent abuse at the hands of her stepmother. While *Ash* does maintain certain aspects of the classic Cinderella tale, it is the way Lo twists the tale that makes it so powerful. Yes, the story has a traditional happy romantic ending, but the fact that it is a lesbian romance between the protagonist and the King's Huntress is what makes the novel so compelling. Despite the historical setting and the traditional gender roles that most females inhabit in the novel, there are distinct aspects to the novel that deconstruct reader expectations about sex and gender.

When readers enter the story, Ash is still living with her mother and father, as well as fairies, greenwitches, and philosophers. It is a fanciful setting, full of invisible creatures, magic, and, importantly, luminous men in the forest. It is one of those luminous men that tries to draw Ash into a relationship, or is it a deal? It is not really clear, but the plotline is a certain reference to the tradition of heterosexual relationships being somewhat dangerous and, perhaps, unhealthy for young girls. When Ash first meets the mysterious and luminous Sidhean in the woods, she is strangely attracted to him and his somewhat controlling behavior. At one point Sidhean warns Ash against her own transgressive behavior, noting she is somewhat reckless in her abandonment of boundaries. He tells her: "Every time you come near me … you come closer to the end of everything" (125). This pronouncement seems odd, since the relationship they are developing appears a caring one (albeit, paternalistic) or potentially even one of a romantic nature. How could such a relationship mark the "end of everything"? In the overall trajectory of Ash's journey her attraction to

Sidhean becomes overshadowed by her new attraction to the King's Huntress, Kaisa. The resulting implication is that if Ash settles into a "bargain" (some might argue that is what traditional marriage in part is) with Sidhean, she will lose her freedom and her ability to roam the woods and hunt with Kaisa, whom, it is clear, she adores.

Ash plays with tradition in ways that contemporary settings do not allow. The young protagonist is free to roam the woods (a metaphor here for sexual exploration) and free to enjoy relationships with men and women without reprisal. Her only constraint is her indentured servitude to her nasty stepmother, but even then Ash is helped by others to continue to roam free. While the freedom to love and follow one's heart is the overarching theme in *Ash*, the question of what one might have to give up to do so is critical. Though *Ash* manages to twist a classic tale in a way that makes same sex attraction seem less insurmountable than the inextricable bonds of heterosexual romance, it is not accomplished without first having to mask the true self before arriving at a self-definition requiring strife, confinement, and even bereavement. Again, *Ash* presents a concept of femininity not easily pinned on a pre-determined spectrum. Who is Ash when in disguise? When in the woods with Sidhean? When on the hunt with Kaisa? The answers are sometimes ambiguous and in flux until the very end.

One final set of important texts that could be added to a list of relevant stories meant to challenge gender norms are two graphic novels depicting young women in formation. The first, *Skim* (2008), is a remarkable and beautifully rendered coming of age graphic narrative, created by cousins Mariko Tamaki (words) and Jillian Tamaki (drawings). It is the story of Kim Cameron, nicknamed Skim because, as she herself notes, "slim" she is not. This story is told through Skim's perspective in a diary format, and since she is also an artist, much of what the reader learns about her is conveyed through image as well as text. It is through many of these images that the ways Skim resists gender norms and traditional femininity are portrayed. Also, some of the most moving moments from the novel are conveyed solely through drawings. For example, no text at all accompanies a two-page drawing of Skim and a friend waiting silently and hopefully in the forest for the conjured up ghost of their deceased friend John to appear.

Likewise, when Skim accidentally meets her English teacher in the woods one day (both are sneaking cigarettes), it is clear through the drawings that Skim feels some kind of new attraction toward the teacher, Ms. Archer. As their friendship develops, there is eventually a double page drawing showing Skim and Ms. Archer kissing. Skim says nothing in her diary about the kiss, but the pictures say what she cannot articulate in words. As the story progresses, it allows Skim to develop her same sex feelings for Ms. Archer in a nonjudgmental way, depicting her desire, depression, anxiety, and wonder at her newly found feelings. Eventually, Ms. Archer leaves the school, seemingly to avoid any further contact with Skim. Skim is forced to move on, sad at first, but eventually developing a close friendship with a young woman named Katie. The last image of the novel is of Skim meeting Katie in the woods, presumably for another, more feasible romantic moment.

It is somewhat remarkable and definitely notable that this graphic narrative makes absolutely no judgment on Skim's presumed sexual orientation. Readers are free to examine Skim's development as a process of self-awareness rather than one of struggle and pain related only to her sexual orientation. Although at one point Skim writes in her diary that "Being sixteen is officially the worst thing I've ever been" (103), her morose pronouncement seems appropriate to a teenager's usual trials and tribulations and not limited to issues of sexuality. Also remarkable is that Skim's weight is never mentioned aside from her teacher's inquiry into her nickname. Skim is a big girl, and that is that. In the twenty-first century it is almost miraculous to read a story about a teenage girl who does not fit the body "norm" but who also does not seem concerned about it. Her weight is not a problem in this novel, the narrative clearly suggesting that no one takes issue with Skim's weight, not even Skim herself. One of the things this novel does so beautifully well is to stay true to the first person narration of Skim's experience of her own life. While the interlude with the teacher is certainly shocking to some, the way it is handled is from Skim's perspective, so recrimination from the outside and authority figures is not the point. This focus is essential for teen readers—to move the narrative to some kind of punishment for the teacher's transgression would certainly feel like a betrayal to the heart and soul of Skim's story and development.

Finally, a YA graphic novel concerning the dismantling of gender norms that deserves attention is Lynda Barry's *Cruddy* (1999). *Cruddy* depicts the short and tragic life of Roberta Rohbeson, a young woman whose brief existence includes being abandoned by her mother, dragged around the country by her father, molestation by a random stranger, and the befriending of a ragtag bunch of misfit teenagers who join her in an adventure to find a suitcase full of money. While *Cruddy* may not seem like a typical YA novel (and it certainly is not typical of anything, really), it has many attributes that make the YAL label difficult to reject. And while the easy way out may be to reject this novel as inappropriate for teens, I would argue that we need to allow teens to read freely. YAL is certainly one of the most monitored categories of reading material in existence. Further surveillance of teens and what they read is the last thing we need as a culture; instead, our attention should be placed on what teens think about when they read complex texts. As Tison Pugh writes in the introduction to *Innocence, Heterosexuality, and the Queerness of Children's Literature*:

> To surveil the child is to discipline the child, and children's literature plays a pivotal role in this process, with narratives instructing their readers in proper or improper citizenship yet doing so in a manner in which their lessons can be dismissed, if necessary. (7)

In Pugh's view, we must consider *Cruddy* an acceptable read for teens who choose it, despite its violence, focusing instead on what meaning can be made of the story rather than the appropriateness of it.

Cruddy is remarkable for many reasons, notwithstanding the violence, but truly because of the resilience and strength of Roberta. Roberta is one of the most powerful adolescent female characters in all of fiction, and her resistance to social norms and gender constraints is a potent challenge to the dominant cultural view of what it means to be a female adolescent. Told from Roberta's perspective by means of a journey that begins when she is eleven and ends when she is sixteen, *Cruddy* includes many episodes that might shock readers, but ultimately it is its story of hope and resilience that makes it important. I have included Roberta's narrative because although she is not identified as a lesbian, her character is one of the most gender-troubling I have read anywhere. Roberta describes herself as extremely ugly, with a chipped tooth and various other disfigurements. Her own father renames her "Clyde" and pretends she is a boy for his own nefarious purposes. When Roberta describes herself, she does it by describing what she once looked like in an old picture:

> The picture was of the very olden me, my hair very very short, shaved like a boy's and my arms and legs so skinny and my expression very paralyzed, me holding Cookie in my breadstick arms. (14)

Roberta's vision of herself, framed by her contemporary self, reveals so much about how she is viewed by the world and especially her father. Roberta also describes herself in a later sequence: "I have looked like a boy since the beginning of forever, a pug-ugly one was how the father said it. Unusually ugly" (60). Yet throughout her narrative Roberta maintains and fosters a sense of herself as a valuable human being, despite being labeled "a dog" (60), which many females know as one of the worst possible insults to be hurled at a girl.

Roberta's gender bending is not deliberate on her part—she just is the way she is. But somehow that fact connects to readers in that many young women feel as if they are the way they are and there is nothing that can change them. One of the most significant aspects of Roberta's story is not only the acceptance of her own appearance, but also that of another young woman she finds herself in a relationship with, Vicky Talluso, whom Roberta describes for readers:

> She had slightly bulged-out eyes with a lot of violet eye shadow and globbed-on mascara and she had a long nose that humped up in the middle and white frosted lipstick coated thick on very chapped lips and her lips protruded forward because her twisted eyeteeth bucked-out, a defect that was weirdly alluring. (19)

Roberta and Vicky are very close, bonded by circumstance and shared exclusion from the popular crowd in their school. They are most definitely "queer," yet they are not romantically involved. Their friendship signifies the power and influence homosocial bonding can have in a coming of age narrative, and certainly both

Roberta and Vicky are bonded by their unique positions on the spectrum of femininity, once again presenting challenges to ideals of beauty, femininity, and gender.

The Spectrum of Femininity in Practice

In constructing a spectrum of femininity, whether in a group or for individual consideration, it is useful first to define what femininity means. The dictionary definition, personal definitions, and definitions by consensus are all productive ways to start a conversation about gender norm expectations. As mentioned earlier, ideally it would be most useful if, for classroom study, students could create their own spectrum of femininity. There are myriad ways this exercise can be facilitated, and certainly there are many books other than the ones mentioned that can provide serious consideration of the issue.

After defining femininity, a first step toward a spectrum would be, either in small or large groups, to list words that might fit onto the spectrum. The words students come up with should not be constrained or limited, but should still be carefully selected. It is likely that certain words and phrases will always be included, such as: girly, frilly, soft, passive, strong, active, powerful, weak, pretty, ugly, aggressive, loud, quiet, obedient, respectful, attractive, big, small, shapely, shrill, silent, smooth, rough, sharp, fast, slow, and perhaps nurturing. Again, these adjectives should not be considered the only acceptable words to use on a spectrum, but they may constitute a good place to start.

Ideally, the class spectrum would be created on a large surface with an organizing template (such as the rainbow described in my opening remarks) where everyone could see and contribute to the process. It might also be useful or more feasible in certain circumstances to have each student create individual spectrums, especially in situations where self-reflection may be the only viable option for consideration of nonstereotypical issues of gender. It would also prove useful to create spectrums at the beginning of each term or semester and return to them regularly to map evolving and new characters that challenge or reinforce views of what it means to be feminine. It might also be interesting and useful to include novel-to-film representations of femininity for discussion. For example, when Laurie Halse Anderson's 1999 novel *Speak* was made into a movie, the film version included some radical changes to the way Melinda, the protagonist, was depicted. In the novel she is an average looking, size 12 girl, but in the 2004 film the lovely and slender Kristen Stewart, well known for playing Bella in the *Twilight* films, plays Melinda. Comparing the two depictions could be very useful in a discussion about the standard of beauty, femininity, and sexuality acceptable not only in text but at the box office as well.

Another approach to creating and reinforcing a consideration of a spectrum of femininity would be to integrate the construction of the spectrum into the reading process itself. As students read, they can underline or write down aspects or attributes of characters they consider relevant to the spectrum. Once their reading is done, they would work to identify certain characteristics, picking and choosing from the chosen attributes and then determining where they fall on the spectrum. Lastly, discussion considerations that help facilitate the formation of ways to "read" femininity in texts of any type would be important. Here are some sample starter ideas for large or small groups:

1. Describe your chosen female character using adjectives that are accurate but not judgmental.

    a. List the adjectives chosen from left to right, with left being most stereo-typically feminine, moving toward the middle to include gender neutral terms, and gradually placing the least stereotypically feminine descriptors to the right.

    b. Choose three adjectives from the range that seem the most significant for your character. What do those words suggest about her? How is her character defined by these attributes?

2. Choose three words from your spectrum that you see as relating to sexuality and sexual orientation. How do these words (in particular) suggest attributes of femininity and sexuality? Could they be gender neutral? Try to imagine which terms could be applied to males. What would these terms suggest if used to describe male characters?

3. Choose a male character from the novel just as you did a female character. List a few adjectives that seem to describe his "gendered" qualities. Can any of these terms be used to describe female characters? How do they differ when used regarding females? Do they suggest something derogatory or positive?

4. What kinds of positive messages does it appear that certain terms suggest? What kinds of negative messages do other terms suggest? What kinds of words can be used to convey different gender configurations?

5. Go back to making an original list of adjectives for a chosen female character. How does her character challenge what it means to be feminine in the twenty-first century?

It is no small feat in our patriarchal and hetero-normative culture to be able to attempt such a transformative reading practice; but, through the process of reading about and perhaps identifying with unique and quirky female characters, it is possible that girls may be able to see themselves in terms of being "constructed" in our culture and learn how to break out of that construct if so desired. This process of recognizing that gender and femininity are both constructions of culture may be a bit complex for some young women, but it is imperative to note that it is not outside the boundaries of what we can expect young women to understand and, perhaps, at the very least, might encourage them to recognize, in the interest of self-development, acceptance, and social change.

Works Cited

American Education Research Association. *Call for Research on GLBT Issues.* http://www. aera.net/Default.aspx?id=10578, 2010. Web.

Association for Middle Level Education. *Association for Middle Level Education.* http://www. amle.org/moya/Partners/tabid/1173/Default.aspx, 2010. Web.

Barry, Lynda. *Cruddy.* New York: Simon and Schuster, 1999. Print.

Fitzhugh, Louise. *Harriet the Spy.* New York: Harper & Row, 1964. Print.

Garden, Nancy. *Annie on My Mind.* New York: Farrar, Straus and Giroux, 1982. Print.

Inness, Sherrie. *The Lesbian Menace.* Amherst: University of Massachusetts Press, 1997. Print.

Lo, Malinda. *Ash.* New York: Little, Brown and Company, 2009. Print.

Meixner, Emily. "Would You Want to Read That? Using Book Passes to Open up Secondary Classrooms to LGBTQ Young Adult Literature." *The ALAN Review* 36.3 (2009): 92–98. Print.

Myracle, Lauren. *Kissing Kate.* New York: Penguin, 2003. Print.

National Council of Teachers of English. *Resolution on Strengthening Teacher Knowledge of Lesbian, Gay, Bisexual, and Transgender (LGBT) Issues.* http://www.ncte.org/positions/ statements/teacherknowledgelgbt, 2007. Web.

Peters, Julie Anne. *Keeping You a Secret.* New York: Little, Brown and Company, 2003. Print.

Pipher, Mary. *Reviving Ophelia.* New York: G.P. Putnam's Sons, 1994. Print.

Pugh, Tison. *Innocence, Heterosexuality, and the Queerness of Children's Literature.* New York: Routledge, 2011. Print.

Ryan, Sara. *Empress of the World.* New York: Penguin, 2001. Print.

Tamaki, Mariko and Jillian Tamaki. *Skim.* Toronto: Groundwood Books, 2008. Print.

Turner, William. *A Genealogy of Queer Theory.* Philadelphia: Temple University Press, 2000. Print.

5

GIRLS AROUND THE GLOBE AS ADVOCATES FOR POLITICAL, CULTURAL, AND SOCIAL LITERACY AT HOME

Mary Napoli

> I believe stories have this power—they enter us, they transport us, they change things inside us, so invisibly, so minutely, that sometimes we're not even aware that we come out of a great book as a different person from the person we were when we began reading it. (Julia Alvarez)

As described in Alvarez's quote, stories have the power to shape our understanding of the world. Alvarez herself provides many characters whose words and actions inspire and provide insight into the human spirit. Reading and responding to such literature can guide teen readers to think critically about the larger world while enabling the intellectual and emotional development necessary for understanding the world immediately inhabited. I especially believe that the female characters of YA global literature have the power to encourage girls to look at their own life stories in new ways. As Louise Rosenblatt notes: "As the student shares, through literary experiences, the emotions and aspirations of other human beings, she/he can gain heightened sensitivity to the needs and problems of those remote from her/him in temperament, in space, or in social environment" (24).

YAL that embodies strong female protagonists who act with courage and compassion to bring about change not only allows readers to consider socio-political and cultural issues but also holds transformative power to help them recognize how to engage or participate in social justice through self-action. By inviting teens to dialogue about global factors that affect all societies through books they can personally relate to, educators invite them to become agents of change as they discover egregious circumstances that exist across borders. Literature gives momentum to the possibility of lifting people up and developing their consciousness. When we read powerful stories, we see not only through the eyes of the characters but also through eyes that are able to see new worlds. Such stories have the power to launch

social and political conversations, not necessarily with an agenda to change someone, but rather with the aim of coming to deeper recognitions of the full humanity
of self and others. As Susan Colby and Anna Lyon point out, "global literature can
help children to identify with their own culture, expose children to other cultures,
and open the dialogue on issues regarding diversity" (24).

In this chapter, I explore how global YAL provides teachers and students with
an important site to consider issues of freedom, courage, and justice. Particularly,
I discuss research conducted while facilitating a summer book club with a group of
six teen girls in the 7th and 8th grade. Over a two-month period, we met regularly
at a local community center in Central Pennsylvania. As part of our activity, we
read selections from a global text set intended to bridge conversations about how
we read the world, celebrate differences, and connect to texts in broad and personal
ways. I was especially interested in the girls' responses to texts whose characters
overcome obstacles and odds under circumstances that the girls in the club might
never experience, but whose situations might vicariously help the girls better
understand privileged stances and undue injustices.

One particular sunny day, a gentle breeze was so inviting that the group decided
to sit outside to talk about responses to *The Diary of Ma Yan: The Struggles and Hopes
of a Chinese Schoolgirl*. While making our way outside, Julia, typically quite reticent,
shared that she was tired of how the media does not share all the real stories that
happen around the world. When asked to elaborate, she said:

> Well, I think that it is really sad that we don't hear about the stories about
> real teens in the world unless a teacher wants us to read a book or news
> article or maybe see a news segment, but it is really not something we talk
> about. I know that me and my friends have things pretty good after reading
> the stories we've been talking about. Maybe we have to write letters to see if
> we can get these books to read and talk about in school.

Julia's comments resonated with the other participants, allowing a chance to talk
about caring for others and issues of fairness and justice. Her critique underscores
the importance of inviting students to respond to and discuss global literature as a
way to "forge a sense of interconnectedness and community so that the community
is one pervaded by attitudes of open-mindedness and respect" (Stallworth 478) and
to "challenge educators to consider engagements with books that build intercultural
understanding, not stereotypes" (Short et al. 131). The thoughtful dialogue and
exchange around just this one piece of literature provided an expanded opportunity
for these teens to reflect upon their own cultural experiences and to consider the
global circumstances of others.

Meeting the Girls

The girls who consistently participated in the club liked to read literature as well as
talk about their lives. Their conversations often included discussion about popular

television shows, movies, music, and dating. Based on the reading survey and personal interviews I conducted, I learned that, for the most part, the girls were average students from suburban and urban settings. Their initial attitudes toward reading varied, as did their exposure to YA global texts, whether read privately or in school. Table 5.1 provides brief information about each active participant.

Even though the girls were from various social and economic backgrounds, they wanted to participate in a community with other girls to talk about stories. Given the history of book clubs, the fact that girls are more likely to participate is not surprising (Long 42). Adolescent girls often articulate the desire for space to relax and laugh, explore emerging identities as young women, and develop a sense of personal integrity (Pastor et al. 15). When asked why they wanted to participate in the book club, the girls agreed it was just a good place to talk about books with other girls. Throughout the meetings, they formed friendships, exchanged phone numbers and email addresses, and met on social media pages. Two of the girls realized they would be in the same homeroom at the beginning of the new year, and two mentioned they did not live far from each other.

Creating a Space

It is my concern for social justice and equity for all students that led me to explore the tenets of critical literacy and reader response theory with the girls as they read selections for the book club. I believe education should be transformative for both the individual and the society, and one of its overarching goals should be to develop caring and compassionate citizens who appreciate and respect the larger world. Thus, I was excited about the opportunity to share global literature with this group of interested teen girls. My first endeavor was to create an atmosphere of trust and openness, so the girls would know that their perspectives, culture, and language were valued and respected. It was clear to me early on that the wider world of the participants extended well beyond the boundaries of our meeting place, across neighborhoods and communities, and into the girls' homes. Their link to these worlds was also the "language universe of their elders" (Freire 31). Giroux points out that today's students, like those in the book club, "no longer belonged to any one place or location, [they] increasingly inhabited shifted cultural and social spheres marked by a plurality of languages and cultures" (88). These girls in particular represented a variety of cultures, and they self-identified in the following ways: African American (Shadra and Monique), African American/Puerto Rican (Julia), Caucasian (Ivy), Asian American (Sarah), and Latina American (Dominique). Each girl brought different ways of knowing the world that dynamically interconnected to their reading of the word (Freire 31) through global literature.

The club met for literature circles on a weekly basis, and each meeting was approximately 60–75 minutes in length. Harvey Daniels' work with literature circles reinforces the importance of implementing discussion in the classroom and beyond, which is perhaps the most essential ingredient for igniting the interest of

TABLE 5.1 The Girls

Pseudonym	Age	Ethnicity	Family Structure	Self-descriptors from Interview/Survey
Shadra	13	African American	Parents divorced; lives with mother and siblings.	Active in sports and music. Mother was sixteen when she was born and doesn't want same thing to happen to her. Very vocal. Doesn't censor thoughts about issues.
Monique	14	African American	Parents recently divorced; lives with mother and grandmother.	Participating to supplement summer reading requirements. Has mixed attitudes about reading. Had negative early grade school and reading experiences based on troubled home life. Beginning to like school again, but still struggles with reading. Likes sports, movies, and fashion.
Julia	13	African American/ Puerto Rican	Lives with both parents and two younger siblings.	Quiet. Loves books and movies based on books. Very good student (As and Bs). Likes music. Likes to paint.
Sarah	14	Asian American	Lives with both parents, maternal grandmother and one older sister.	Well-liked by friends and classmates. Treasurer of student government. Loves animals. Loves to travel (has traveled domestically and internationally to Europe, Asia, and Australia). Loquacious and good sense of humor.
Dominique	13	Latina American	Father deceased, lives with mother and grandmother and four siblings.	Recently moved back to area. Father recently died in combat overseas. Mom travels a lot for work. Loves to write (found peace through writing when her dad was away). Enjoys poetry. Likes cooking and race cars.
Ivy	14	Caucasian	Parents divorced; both recently remarried. Lives with mother and four siblings.	Avid reader. Loves music and playing computer games. Loves horseback riding. Likes swimming and animals.

young adolescent readers (15). Literature circles are popular because they encourage reading as a social activity, creating a space where readers can share their experiences with literature and discuss connections as well as differences between readers and characters. Within this setting, readers use books and one another's responses "to promote insight and empathy in an integrative process of collective self-reflection (Long 145). Hill et al. suggest that literature circles should be formed on the basis of students' selections (10), an approach I embrace and used with the girls in the club. After getting started with a couple of novels I thought the girls would enjoy, I provided multiple copies of several novels and then invited students to choose the books they wanted to read. By doing so, the girls then began discussions guided by their own insights, observations, and questions. Through this dialogue, different interpretations and understandings were constructed and multiple meanings shared.

Although the book club was open to everyone, the participants included in this study were consistently present throughout the entire two-month period, and their parent(s) or guardian(s) agreed to their participation in the study. Reader response journals were used to record the girls' feelings, reflections, and reactions to the texts. This interaction between reader and text extended their reading experience into the "real life" application of information. The girls also responded to their chosen novels through tableaux, art, music, and media.

After the conclusion of the last book club session, I conducted and transcribed semi-structured interviews with all of the girls in order to obtain individual per-spectives about the literature we had read as a community and to examine their thinking behind the transactions with literacy that encompassed learning about the larger world. Although there have been several studies about the relationship between literacy and female gender identity construction and responses to literature (Blackford; Cherland; Finders), there are few studies about how teen girls respond to global literature and issues of justice.

As noted, to get us reading immediately, I selected the first two books. I then conducted book talks and shared digital book trailers for several other selections, inviting the girls to nominate and choose texts they wanted to read. In addition to reading seven YA novels, the girls also recommended and nominated non-fiction titles, movies, and poetry. Expanding the traditional understanding of "text" pro-vided opportunities for the girls to share their preferences and identities as readers while acknowledging the multiple ways we gain meaning through print or visual media. During each book club meeting, we discussed the content, characters, and themes of our books. Table 5.2 provides a list of the literature selected by the girls and me for reading and discussion.

In our meetings, the girls exchanged journals and, depending on the theme, responded through multiple sign systems, such as drama, art, music, and technology. Though my role was that of organizer and facilitator, as a former teacher and now teacher educator, I brought the experience of working with readers of different ages and backgrounds to the club, which allowed me to submerge myself in the com-munity culture, an integral factor in qualitative research (Ely et al. 31). I also made

TABLE 5.2 Literature Selections

Book	Author	Overall Themes	Selection Process	Summary
The Other Side of Truth (2000) [Nigeria]	Beverly Naidoo	*authoritarian governments *lawlessness *immigration and issues of political asylum *courage *family *power of truth *injustices *freedom of speech *human rights *political impact on the young *bullying	Researcher (me)	As Sade prepares for school, she hears gunfire shots. She learns her mother has been murdered. Fearing for the safety of his children, Sade's father quickly arranges for them to be smuggled into England. After arriving, they are abandoned and left on their own to survive.
Year of Impossible Goodbyes (1991) [Korea]	Sook Nyul Choi	*love, cruelty, and suffering *Second World War from a different perspective *hope and determination in dark times *impact of war on the young *the human spirit *tolerance and compassion	Researcher (me)	This novel is about Sookan and her family's determination to find freedom. It's based on the author's childhood experiences in Korea near the end of WWII.

TABLE 5.2 (CONTINUED)

Book	Author	Overall Themes	Selection Process	Summary
Our Secret, Siri Aang (2004) [Kenya]	Cristina Kessler	* social tradition * conflicts * identity/self-discovery * cultural values * change and assimilation * transitioning into womanhood * conservation and ecology * coming of age	Girls	Namelok, a Maasai girl, lives in Kenya. She is being prepared for initiation into womanhood. Namelok questions the cultural practice, but eventually accepts the tradition. One day, she watches a black mother rhino give birth and tries to keep both creatures safe from poachers.
Before We Were Free (2002) [Dominican Republic]	Julia Alvarez	* self-discovery * racial prejudice * poverty * family relationships * survival * political freedom * culture and society * oppression	Girls	In the early 1960s, in the Dominican Republic, Anita learns that her family is involved in a movement to end the rule of The Dictator General el Trujillo.
Tree Girl (2004) [Central America, Guatemala]	Ben Mikaelsen	* refugees * self-knowledge * war and conflict * equity, fairness, justice * self-reliance * rebellion	Girls	Based on true accounts of one girl's story of survival of the genocide that occurred in Guatemala. Gabriela finds "trust among the trees."

TABLE 5.2 (CONTINUED)

Book	Author	Overall Themes	Selection Process	Summary
Colibrí (2003) [Central America, Guatemala]	Ann Cameron	* social issues * death and loss * family * abuse * imagination * kidnapping * goodness	Girls	This novel is set in Guatemala and finds Colibrí seeking her freedom. Her personal choices strengthen the weak and defeat the strong.
The Diary of Ma Yan: The Struggles and Hopes of a Chinese Schoolgirl (2004) [China]	Ma Yan, edited by Pierre Haski	* poverty * courage * equity and fairness * sacrifice * desire and determination	Girls	This is a first person account of a young girl's poverty-stricken life in rural China. Ma Yan records her struggles to fulfill her dream of an education.

arrangements for snacks, purchased supplies, and took responsibility for arranging access for computer time. Since we met only once a week, we negotiated in advance a reading schedule that consisted of completing one book each week, jotting down "golden lines" (powerful quotations from the literature), and writing entries in reader response journals to bring for discussion.

As facilitator, one of my most important tasks was to provide a safe and respectful atmosphere with a consistent structure. This was essential in terms of creating a nurturing social exchange about the books. Vygotsky emphasizes that teachers must help students develop the necessary tools to function within their social setting, thus assisting them in individually developing a new culture (quoted in Berger 25). Berger equates this to empowering students and helping them find their own voices. Vygotsky's idea of scaffolding can be utilized by those working with students to help them critically utilize higher levels of thinking. In the club, there were times when I had to intervene to make sure everyone's voice was heard or to elicit responses from some of the quieter girls. As bell hooks states: it is a "necessary aspect of self-affirmation not to feel compelled to choose one voice over another, not to claim one as more authentic, but rather to construct social realities that celebrate, acknowledge, and affirm differences" (12). In sum, as the facilitator, I impressed upon the girls that the book club was a safe space to share and grow in their thoughts and experiences, even though I occasionally had to gently shift the conversation back to the heart of the literature selection.

The girls came prepared to each session, as agreed, with journal responses and "golden lines" to share. This helped invite readers to identify what was important to them in the reading and gave them key ideas for discussion that could be easily accessed. "Golden lines," especially, as described by Katherine Schlick Noe and Nancy Johnson, "automatically provide[d] interesting discussion material and [we]re an easy and effective strategy for gathering information" (48). Some general discussion prompts were also shared in order to generate critical reading and thinking around issues of perspective, positioning, and power. Since texts are not simply words on a page but represent sites of struggle and controversy, the girls read and responded to text in part by considering broad based questions such as: Whose interests do the texts serve? Whose experiences, meanings, or viewpoints are omitted? Privileged? What kinds of people/lives/experiences/beliefs are presented? In what ways does the book position readers as insider, outsider, both, or neither? Who has power in the story? Who is silenced or oppressed? How do the girls in the stories demonstrate agency? In what ways do girls act to free themselves from institutions of power and privilege? What about our lives? In what ways have we espoused agency/self-empowerment? By inviting the girls to dialogue about the readings through the thoughtful consideration of various lenses, they were able to think about and articulate beliefs about social issues. As Freire writes, learning is possible through dialogue because "without dialogue, there is no communication, and without communication, there can be no true education" (81). As a community of readers, the girls became navigators and critical text detectives trying to gain a deeper or new understanding of the word and the world. By approaching the texts through a critical framework, a site was provided to extend, build upon, and complicate prior understandings of the world.

In an effort to use literature intended to provide sophisticated thinking and action, the books selected offered excellent opportunities to consider notions of freedom, societal constraints, democracy, agency, and justice. All of the selections received positive reviews from reputable sources such as the *School Library Journal*, *Horn Book*, and *VOYA* (*Voices of Youth Advocates*), with the general consensus being that the texts would bring readers together around respective understandings of various cultures. I felt it especially important in this out-of-school setting to have a set of texts written by authors who used an authentic voice; given the goal of expanding the girls' worldview, I thought it necessary to take into account the author's own cultural and ethnic background.

Author identity and representation have been central considerations in the debate about what global literature is or is not (Cai 312), so as I worked with the girls, we discussed how no one person can speak for or represent an entire group. As Botelho and Rudman note, "we are all outsiders to a degree, unless we are specifically portraying ourselves. And even then our portrayal is a representation of our lived experience" (104). Because I wanted to encourage the girls to continue to select high quality global literature even after our club finished, we discussed the criteria utilized for selection, some of the awards given for exemplary global literature, and useful, recommended websites.

Engaging the Girls in Critical Reading

The girls' readings of the YA selections provide a dramatic way to analyze agency and the concept of social justice while illuminating and contextualizing their world. The obvious challenge was to create a safe space to discuss difficult and sensitive topics and issues, so that critical conversations and dialogue about equity, agency, and justice could be explored. In an effort to supply a framework for engaging the girls in critical readings I established three categories: (1) Global and Cultural Context; (2) Positioning; (3) Care, Justice, and Equity. What follows is a brief example of how the girls handled the conversations around each category. After consideration of each, we take a closer look at the girls' comments on one novel in particular, *The Diary of Ma Yan*.

Global and Cultural Context

Within this lens, the girls were encouraged to think about how global literature shapes and challenges understandings of the world. Historical events as related to specific pieces of literature and cultural context were explored. It became clear that the cultural contexts not only deepened understanding of the cultures the girls were reading about but also caused them to examine their own culture and cultural diversity in general.

MARY: We've been discussing *The Other Side of Truth* and the issue of freedom. What do we think about Sade and Femi's situation as they are heading out of Nigeria into a country that at one time had strong political ties? What are your thoughts in terms of their situation and level of freedom in Nigeria and in London?

SHADRA: I think they didn't have freedom. Sade's brother was quiet and sort of did not want to get into trouble. I did not like that they got bullied by some of the kids in London and were treated poorly.

JULIA: Yeah, I agree. It is not fair that their father was writing about the inequality going on around in his country and then he lost his wife. I didn't like that the kids got bullied after they had to be shipped out of their home. This happens sometimes to my friends and me at lunch—the bullying part—not the freedom. I think that Sade is pretty smart and tries to protect her brother.

DOMINIQUE: This was a tough story for me since it dealt with the death of a loved one and about terrorism. I think that the dad did the best he could, considering he wanted to make sure nothing happened to them. I never really thought about the struggles that children from refugee families had to go through.

Positioning

In this category, the girls interacted with the voices and experiences of empowered female characters and considered how they courageously engaged with the world and their circumstances. Here I would like to consider Seelinger Trites' notion of what adolescents learn about power. She explains that adolescents (in society and in literature) are both powerful and disempowered (xi). Coming-of-age novels present an opportunity for readers to navigate how young female protagonists explore their power through acts of resilience and resistance, how they resist oppressive power, and what empowerment and transformation mean to the characters. Sarah begins the conversation by describing the qualities of the main character:

> Sadie is really smart and strong willed like Julia said. She helped bring her dad's problem to the right people so that they could be together. It isn't fair that she had to do all of this by herself, but she has a really good heart and realizes she has to grow up to survive.

As Ivy responds, she does so by making connections between the text being discussed, other texts, and her own life. She positions herself in the "shoes" of the character while considering her own home issues:

> I sort of think that they were really homesick and I can relate to that, especially when I had to go to camp and deal with all these new kids I didn't know. Her story about being strong and surviving reminds me of *Tree Girl* and Gabrielle.

Monique agrees with Ivy's connection to another book the group has read and, in the following exchange, affirms Ivy's experience while offering another connection to female characters:

> Yeah, true, true. I am like Ivy. I think that if we have to be strong to survive, like Sade and Gabriella, then we do what we have to do. I know that losing someone you love stays with you your entire life, so I bet Sade and Gabrielle got some strength from memories and love they knew from their mom.

This opportunity to dialogue about the positionality of characters while considering their own lives encouraged the girls to recognize their commonalities, thus improving their social awareness across cultural as well as global differences.

Care, Justice, and Equity

Nel Noddings writes that "caring" should be the foundation of the curriculum, including caring for ideas, friends, family, the earth, human-made objects, strangers, and distant others (10). With this in mind, the girls were encouraged to discuss how characters overcome injustices while showing compassion for others. Dominique mentions that she "loved how Sade used the media to get her father out of wrong imprisonment. The media can be pretty one sided, but in this story, it did help make a difference." Monique's statement justifies Dominique's while further noting ways in which action can create change:

> I am so with that, Dominique. You are right girl. The television can help make a difference. Like my grandmother says to me, stay true to yourself and what you believe. She told me a story about her and her friends marching for better benefits at work and they made posters, wrote letters, and got interviewed by television and it made a difference. It worked since they got some benefits. They felt like they were heard.

Sarah offers her own views about getting involved as a way of declaring her sense of agency and reinforcing the need for becoming political. She states:

> I am all about making a difference. That is why, like you know, I joined student government. We try to organize things all the time to help other people. I think it is important for us to work together to make change happen. It doesn't happen fast enough so people get sort of bent out of shape, but sticking with it, things can get better.

These interactions, drawn vicariously from textual issues, intersect the importance of collective and individual civic participation in order to become more socially responsible.

Listening to Girls' Voices

As noted, the girls' interactions and respect for one another almost always start with reactions to the text and characters and then move to personal experiences. Their conversation reveals a growing knowledge about cultural context and injustices while affording them new perspectives about themselves and others. For example, when discussing *The Diary of Ma Yan*, it is clear how issues of poverty and equality really affect the girls. Monique is the first to react to the diary:

> I can't believe that she was not allowed to go to school and that the boys were. She was just one year younger than I am now and it just goes to show you that if you want something bad enough you will do whatever you can to get there. Her mom was pretty much there for her and did what she could to get Ma Yan into school. I love the line *"I have to study hard to make a contribution to my country and my people one day. That is my goal. That is my hope."* (110)
>
> I used to have bad experiences as a kid in school, and I just took it for granted. I didn't know that there were kids in the world who couldn't go to school. I just really like this book. It made me really want to do better in school to do something important to help others in my community, like Ma Yan did.

Shadra agrees, and connects the comment to her own life:

> I loved the story, but I liked the relationship with Ma Yan and her mother. I guess it's because my mom is sacrificing a lot to make sure that I don't end up a teen mom and all, so I sometimes give her a hard time because she is always on my case about getting good grades. I felt kind of bad about how I must have been coming off to her especially after reading this book. Ma Yan really shared her feelings about wanting to go to school and making a difference by being a writer—a journalist.

Ma Yan wrote: "I want to pursue journalism to keep the world informed, to report poverty and real life in this area" (153).

Reflecting on this statement, Shadra adds that she thinks Ma Yan's strength and determination are inspiring. "I just want to bottle up her courage and hope and share it with everyone I meet," she states. Shadra's comment reminds me of Maxine Greene's definition of "social imagination" as "the capacity to invent visions of what should be and what might be in our deficient society, on the streets where we live, and in our schools" (5). Social imagination helps students question how we live and envision a better way, or, as Shadra notes about Ma Yan's courage, it makes students aware of possibilities.

As the conversation continues, Dominique agrees with Shadra and adds that she likes how Ma Yan uses a diary format to express her feelings. Curious, I ask her to elaborate a bit more and to find her favorite entry. Without hesitation, Dominique shares:

> Oh, I liked a lot of them, but I just feel that the diary gave Ma Yan a feeling of importance. She is inspiring and knew that to do something important with her life she would have to overcome being poor and go to school. I just never thought about this view. Okay, let me look for a diary entry that was cool. Oh, here is one on page 101 where she talks about writing.

After the girls and I find the page, we listen as Dominique reads aloud:

> Monday, July 30, 2001
> This afternoon, when I want to start writing in my diary, I can't find my pen … I'm distraught. You're probably going to start laughing. "A pen. What a little thing to get so distressed about!" If you only knew the trouble I had to get that pen … the difficulties I faced in getting this pen are a mirror of all my other problems. My mother had given me some money with which to buy bread. For days I had only eaten yellow rice. I preferred going hungry and saving so that I could buy the pen … my dear old pen gave me the sense of power. It made me understand the meaning of a difficult life or a happy life. Every time I see the pen, it's as if I were seeing my mother. It's as if she was encouraging me to work hard and make it into the girls' senior school. (101)

As the group pauses to savor the beauty of this message, I am curious to hear more about the girls' views about Ma Yan's agency, power, and determination to write. Dominique is the first to share, saying she feels the quote sums up how she feels about writing and that "it is so great to put down your thoughts into words and feel like I have a voice." Ivy continues the conversation, taking it even further by affirming the important place this literature has in the curriculum. Many young people know very little about the world beyond their own neighborhood or state, she says, let alone beyond our country's borders.

> I love that quote too. It makes me appreciate things that I have. I don't know what I'd do if my family couldn't get me the things that I needed. I never realized that there were so many issues around the world. I didn't know that so many girls, like Ma Yan, couldn't go to school and that their families had to struggle to make money to eat. Ma Yan really had to go through a tough time before she could eventually go to school. I mean it is like what she wrote on page 55.
> Wednesday, November 7
> My father gave me and my brother a little money. My stomach is all twisted up with hunger, but I don't want to spend the money on anything as

frivolous as food. Because it's money my parents earn with their sweat and blood. I have to study well so that I won't ever again be tortured by hunger ... (55)

Ivy goes on to say:

> I just feel like I need to be more thankful for what I have. I mean sometimes I don't want to eat the food that my mother makes and I make a big fuss, and so do my brothers and sisters. I think that they need to read this book too. I just didn't realize that other people in other parts of the world had to go through this.

Again, the girls show they are becoming informed citizens on global matters concerning hunger, gender, justice, and education; certainly, they are engaged in the issues of the world.

We talk about the fact that after the diary was published, there was a huge outpouring of support for Ma Yan's courage and story, and that people worked together to develop an international organization (the Association of Children of Ningxia) to help other children in similar circumstances. The girls eagerly explore the issue of making a difference. As Monique states: "That is so awesome. I love that people did something good to help her and other kids around the world. I want to do something like this. Can we do something to make a difference as a group?"

Reflecting upon the overall exchange, it is clear that the girls display the personal and social agency needed to deal with issues in a personal and public manner while retaining the empathy necessary to stay connected to the story characters. The heart-wrenching account of Ma Yan teaches the girls not only about the resolve necessary for perseverance but about social agency as well. They feel safe to share their thoughts on all aspects of Ma Yan's situation, and I am able to model the process of making connections between their lived world experiences and the text (Beach et al. 15). "[G]ranting voice and legitimacy to the perspectives and experiences of those who are different from themselves—communities that do not require students to surrender personal and cultural identity in exchange for academic achievement" (Nelson-Barber and Meir 5) becomes an important tenet of the club. While participating in an open exchange of ideas and feelings about the texts, the girls become better able to consider their own stance in becoming change agents in their own communities.

Responding through Poetry and Multimedia

Through multiple responses to the texts, the girls further extended discussions of agency and the complexities of culture related to personal, social, and global issues. After teaching them how to write found poems, they worked in pairs to create powerful new texts that indicated the depth to which they perceived the issues. Found poetry is not an unknown strategy, but it is a successful way to guide students to learning about how poetry works while engaging them with specifics of a text. As Dunning and Stafford explain, the advantage of found poems is "you don't start from scratch. All you have to do is find some good language and 'improve' it" (3). These two teachers note that "poems hide in things you and others say and write. They lie buried in places where language isn't so self-conscious as 'real poetry' often is. [Writing found poems] is about keeping your ears and eyes alert to the possibilities in ordinary language" (3). Here are two examples of found poems written by the girls that capture the essence of the original stories:

Sarah and Julia: *The Diary of Ma Yan*

Sacrifice
Sweat and hard labor
Work really hard
Poverty
Education
Reading and Writing
Secretly happy
Making a difference
Contribute toward the country
Hope

Dominique and Shadra: *Colibri*

Hummingbird
Flight
Pain in her eyes
Something hidden
Nightmare
White and red butterfly
Flight
Hummingbird

As a teacher educator, I feel it imperative to offer up the tools of technology to the girls in response to a digital world. Employing multimodal responses allows students to work across "multiple sign systems" (Short et al. 35) and use a variety of strategies to navigate, interpret, and comprehend texts. As the girls read *Year of Impossible Goodbyes*, they are invited to think about symbols, images, colors, pictures, music, video, quotes, short phrases, and different designs to create a multimodal response. Included here in Figure 5.1 is Julia and Sarah's response.

Figure 1
Year of Impossible Goodbyes
Multimodal Response by Julia and Sarah

Cultural Symbols
Tree, lunch box, traditional
silk clothing, silver hair clip,

"Darkness and light, peace and joy, evil and good. All these tensions and conflicts were necessary in the struggle for perfect harmony." Sookan

H
O
P
E

Because I was a girl, I was supposed to stay with the women. I wasn't supposed to disturb Grandfather after my morning lesson. How I wished I could be with them" (10)

Family history is important.
Sookan's mother shares lots of
photos.

FIGURE 5.1 Multimodal Response

I believe that reading and sharing global literature through a variety of lenses has the potential to help readers recognize in more depth the specificity of issues in a text while allowing them to connect their own personal and cultural backgrounds to the contexts of others. As Jeff Wilhelm states, students need time to construct meanings from text: "When readings are shared, students have the opportunity to create responses together, to compare responses and ways of reading and to learn from each other about these ways of reading" (73). Within the book club the girls experienced shared dialogue, social awareness, and respect. Through their written responses, they were able to interrogate the text from different perspectives and reflect upon their own lives, resulting in meaningful and authentic transactions.

Final Thoughts

Exploring global texts and discussing them within a community provide an opportunity to gain multiple perspectives while reading critically and widely about the world. Despite the obvious limitations of what can be accomplished in two months, the book club did allow the girls to read high quality selections of literature with a new perspective. As Joan Kaywell et al. note: "YAL can provide a variety of lenses through which to view the adolescent female condition and can help broaden the awareness of its readers" (69). This successful experience serves as a model for those interested in ways to engage girls in reading about other cultures. Weaving in critical questions that problematize texts helps readers gain deeper insights while allowing personal connections and understandings of agency. Such discussions turn reading experiences into sites where the awareness of concepts of justice, equity, and human rights can be enhanced and deepened. As Ivy eloquently explains: "Reading global books gives you a different vision of how you see the world. It teaches you to appreciate the little things you have and try to work harder to make the world a better place."

Works Cited

Alvarez, Julia. *Before We Were Free*. New York: Knopf, 2002. Print.

——"On Becoming a Butterfly." Appalachian State University-Boone, North Carolina, May 2004. Lecture.

Beach, Richard, Deborah Appleman, Susan Hynds, and Jeffrey Wilhelm. *Teaching Literature to Adolescents*. 2nd ed. New York: Routledge, 2010. Print.

Berger, Peter L. *Many Globalizations: Cultural Diversity in the Contemporary World*. Oxford: Oxford University Press, 2002. Print.

Blackford, Holly. *Out of This World: Why Literature Matters to Girls*. New York: Teachers College Press, 2004. Print.

Botelho, Maria José, and Masha Kabakow Rudman, eds. *Critical Multicultural Analysis of Children's Literature: Mirrors, Windows, and Doors*. New York: Routledge, 2009. Print.

Cai, Mingshui. "Multiple Definitions of Multicultural Literature: Is the Debate Really Just 'Ivory Tower' Bickering?" *The New Advocate* 11.4 (1998): 311–24. Print.

Cameron, Ann. *Colibri*. New York: Random House, 2003. Print.

Cherland, Meredith Rogers. *Private Practices: Girls Reading Fiction and Constructing Identity*. London: Taylor and Francis, 1994. Print.

Choi, Sook Nyul. *Year of Impossible Goodbyes*. New York: Random House, 1991. Print.

Colby, Susan A. and Anna F. Lyon. "Heightening Awareness about the Importance of Using Multicultural Literature," *Multicultural Education* 11.3 (2004): 24–28. Print.

Daniels, Harvey. *Literature Circles: Voice and Choice in Book Clubs and Reading Groups*. 2nd ed. Portland, OR: Stenhouse, 2002. Print.

Dunning, Stephen and William Stafford. *Found and Headline Poems. Getting the Knack: 20 Poetry Writing Exercises*. Urbana, IL: NCTE, 1992. Print.

Ely, Margot, Margaret Anzul, Teri Freidman, Diane Garner, and Ann McCormack-Steinmetz. *Doing Qualitative Research: Circles within Circles*. New York: Routledge, 1991. Print.

Finders, Margaret J. *Just Girls: Hidden Literacies and Life in Junior High*. New York: Teachers College Press, 1997. Print.

Freire, Paulo. *Pedagogy of the Oppressed*. New York: Continuum Press, 1970. Print.

Giroux, Henry A. *Border Crossings: Cultural Workers and the Politics of Education*. New York: Routledge, 1992. Print.

Greene, Maxine. *Releasing the Imagination: Essays on Education, the Arts, and Social Change*. San Francisco, CA: Jossey-Bass, 1995. Print.

Hill, Bonnie Campbell, Katherine L. Schlick Noe, and Janine A. King. *Literature Circles in the Classroom: One Teacher's Journey*. Norwood, MA: Christopher-Gordon Publishers, 2003. Print.

hooks, bell. *Talking Back: Thinking Feminist, Thinking Black*. Boston, MA: Second End Press, 1999. Print.

Kaywell, Joan A., Patricia Kelly, Christi Edge, Larissa McCoy, and Narisa Steinberg. "Growing up Female around the Globe with Young Adult Literature." *The ALAN Review* 33.3 (2006): 62–69. Print.

Kessler, Cristina. *Our Secret, Siri Aang*. New York: Philomel, 2004. Print.

Long, Elizabeth. *Book Clubs: Women and the Uses of Reading in Everyday Life*. Chicago, IL: University of Chicago Press, 2003. Print.

Mikaelsen, Ben. *Tree Girl*. New York: HarperCollins, 2004. Print.

Naidoo, Beverly. *The Other Side of Truth*. New York: HarperCollins, 2000. Print.

Nelson-Barber, Sharon and Scott T. Meir. "Multicultural Context: A Key Factor in Teaching." *Academic Connections* 1.5 (1990): 9–11. Print.

Noddings, Nel. *The Challenge to Care in Schools: An Alternative Approach to Education*. New York: Teachers College Press, 1991. Print.

Pastor, Jennifer, Jennifer McCormick, and Michelle Fine. "Makin' Homes: An Urban Girl Thing." *Urban Girls: Resisting Stereotypes, Creating Identities*. Eds. Bonnie J. Ross Leadbeater and Niobe Way. New York: New York University Press, 1996. 15–34. Print.

Rosenblatt, Louise. *Literature as Exploration*. New York: The Modern Language Association of America, 1983. Print.

Short, Kathy, Jerome Harste, and Carolyn Burke. *Creating Classrooms for Authors and Inquirers*. 2nd ed. Portsmouth: Heinemann, 1995. Print.

Stallworth, Brenda Joyce. "It's Not on the List: An Exploration of Teachers' Perspectives on Using Multicultural Literature." *Journal of Adolescent and Adult Literacy* 49.6 (2006): 478–89. Print.

Trites, Roberta Seelinger. *Disturbing the Universe: Power and Repression in Adolescent Literature*. Iowa City: University of Iowa Press, 2000. Print.

Wilhelm, Jeffrey D. *"You Gotta BE the Book": Teaching Engaged and Reflective Reading with Adolescents*. 2nd ed. New York: Teachers College Press, 2008. Print.

Yan, Ma and Pierre Haski. *The Diary of Ma Yan: The Struggles and Hopes of a Chinese Schoolgirl*. New York: HarperCollins, 2004. Print.

6

GIRLS COMPOSING THEIR LIVES

Reading and Writing Contemporary Memoir

Dawn Latta Kirby

Young Adult Literature (YAL) has a long history of engaging readers and of reflecting the world far and near to those who read it. Fiction has dominated what young adults read for several decades, causing some adults to wonder if teens will balk at reading anything else. We know young adults may go through a poetry phase. They may read religious works and holy texts. They may read magazines that appeal to special interests such as fashion, Hollywood updates, or perhaps photography. But will teens engage with nonfiction in as intense a manner as they absorb fiction? This central question has driven much of my professional inquiry over the last twenty or more years.

A Snapshot of Girls and Contemporary Literacy

Hunched over her keyboard, Danielle—a fifteen-year-old student—types faster than some courtroom stenographers. She posts to her blog, sends instant messages, emails friends, plays an interactive computer game, and wears headphones in order to Skype with a friend who lives just four miles away. These activities are virtually—metaphorically and technologically—simultaneous activities. Danielle also pursues other social electronic outlets, such as writing fan fiction based on stories recently read with a group of five to seven of her friends, primarily females, near her age. All the teens regard these activities as highly social, primary ways to connect with peers. What Danielle and her friends read and write on the computer provides fodder for conversations before, during, and after school. It is important to note that many of the genres and venues in which they are highly literate did not exist, quite literally, fifteen or so years ago.

Danielle and her friends engage in myriad literacy activities on their computers for an average of two hours per weekday. The time may triple during the weekend.

Cell phones, though owned and carried everywhere, are almost too dated for this group. They like being able to shift from one activity to another with the quick click of a mouse, showing four quadrants on their over-sized computer screens at all times. This tech stuff is fun. It is what teens like Danielle do to unwind during their free time, refocus after staying late at school, or refuel mentally after hours spent completing school projects. No doubt, this description of Danielle and her friends sounds typical of teenagers we all know and who populate our schools. They are emblematic of many of today's tech savvy, literate teens.

Literacy Observed: Personalizing Fiction

Over the last two years, Danielle, Courtney, Summer, and Alexis—and, for a decade or more, numerous other middle and high school teens with similar literacy interests and abilities—have been the focus of my research on girls' literacy practices. I began this case study somewhat casually and informally by interviewing the girls named above about their self-selected reading. As the study progressed, I listened to their conversations about books, wrote field notes, read their blogs and fan fiction pieces, and observed their interactions. I then sought patterns and commonalities across their texts, uses of technology, and responses to YAL, including fiction and nonfiction. During the study I interacted regularly with the girls, checked my perceptions against theirs, and maintained an etic stance. My role throughout the study was that of observer, interviewer, and trusted "outsider let in."

One of my first observations was that the interests of these avid readers tended to flow and develop within the group culture of their friends. Most of the girls read at least one novel per week for pleasure. They devoured fiction. During the last eighteen months of the study, the teens displayed evolving interests in both reading and writing. From an initial preference for fantasies of wizards and shape-shifters, survival stories among clans of wolves with an ancient history, and vampiric romances, the girls transitioned to stories of love lost and won by female characters much like themselves. They also found an emerging fascination with dystopic literature, with their favorites being works that depict harsh survival games and unnatural occurrences in the physical world and psychic realm. When I talked with the girls about their reading, they reported seeing bits and pieces of themselves in the characters populating the books they read; they identified with the characters' emotions, dilemmas with friends and parents, personal grit and resolve, and ability to negotiate complex issues and conflicting perspectives.

As I continued to note the girls' literacy interactions, I noticed that they frequently referenced characters from their reading in their conversations and delighted in spontaneously enacting entire scenes from favorite novels. During role–plays, as they call their enactments, the girls followed several recognizable stages of developing sophistication in their virtual and face-to-face games. Initially, they enacted the main ideas and dominant emotions of favorite scenes from a novel popular with the group, creating their own dialogue. Then, they repeatedly read the scenes when not with the group, committing the dialogue and related lines in the novel to memory, until they could smoothly quote the author's written dialogue during their role-plays.

At this stage, the girls also formed writing pairs or triads and pursued their fan fiction plotlines. They mimicked the author's tone, style, characterizations, and emotional tenor, but extended the story to include original written dialogue, descriptions, and exposition. Finally, when they gathered for role-play after engaging in their fan fiction writing, the girls freely combined their writing with that of the author to enact increasingly complex and original stories of their own composition that, nonetheless, retained recognizable elements of the published novel. Throughout this process, the girls discussed among themselves what the characters were doing and feeling, and they easily identified personal experiences and feelings with those of the characters. The stages of *observed literacy engagement* for the girls in the case studies, then, are as follows:

- avidly reading novels the group of friends agreed formally or informally to read;
- role-playing scenes from the novel, improvising dialogue;
- reading favorite scenes until each girl memorized large chunks of published text;
- returning to role-play, quoting almost word-for-word the author's published text;
- going online to write fan fiction, improvising and expanding elements of the published novel in their own words through writing;
- returning to role-play to enact personal versions of the published novel, including memorized sections from the author's original published text and from their own writing in a fan fiction genre;
- discussing the feelings and emotions of the characters, the dips and twists in the plot, as comparable or alien to their own experiences.

These engagements allowed the girls to internalize, personalize, amend, and create text that became layered onto the author's published work and to co-mingle and blend elements of their writing with those of the original text. I refer to this process as that of *palimpsest*, which is any work (i.e., painting, manuscripts) that reveals its history through an examination of the layers of other works beneath the currently visible layer. This practice of layering paintings or manuscripts over earlier works was necessary historically because of the cost and rarity of parchment, canvas, and other materials. For these girls, their work with layering original and created texts reveals high levels of invested time, energy, and personal effort to connect with privileged (favored) fictional texts.

As I noted these stages of development with *personalizing fiction*, I began to question what impact, if any, reading and writing nonfiction would have on the girls' literacy practices. Specifically, my ongoing inquiry into and work with contemporary memoir (Kirby and Kirby, 2007) seemed a plausible bridge between the extensions of published works the girls were already composing and the connections they made to their lived experiences within socially connected creative spaces. The focus of my inquiry shifted from their interactions with popular fiction to their level of connectedness with the topics, life situations, authorial tone, and writing techniques frequently used in contemporary memoir written for and read by young adults.

Contemporary Memoir (CM)

On any given week, the *New York Times* Bestseller List is sure to name one or more memoirs. Memoir dates its origins to A.D. 397 with the work of Augustine. Contemporary Memoir (CM), however, has evolved from the original genre and is traced more recently to *Growing Up* (1982) by journalist Russell Baker. CM has become a postmodern, nonfiction genre of increasing critical and popular note. Traditional memoirs written by historical figures, famous people, and presidents depend upon a personal recounting of historical fact for their appeal. The writers of traditional memoirs are part of a particular era or event that makes them noteworthy beyond most people's everyday lives, and the events about which they write can be literally verified by historical record. In contrast, writers of CM are people who may not be famous at all until their books are published; yet their lived experiences resonate with readers. Have you experienced taking care of a special needs child or aging parent? Have you experienced drug addiction or a religious conversion, or do you know someone who has? Are you just curious about what living in those circumstances must be like? Do you love nature and reading about those who work to preserve it? Are you riveted by accounts from Holocaust survivors? Perhaps you wonder about the lives of those who immigrate to America from other, possibly war-torn countries. If so, a CM no doubt exists to inform you and engage your interest.

Most notably, CM is a tectonic genre. It does not consist of five elements, nor is it bound by strict convention. CMs are as varied in content and style as those who author them. What fascinates readers about CM, however, is the way in which the author's experiences connect with—or serve as an insightful foil to—those of the reader.

Another key feature of CM is that it reads like fiction. Far from being a dry, textbook-like tome, CMs employ many of the literary elements found in fiction, such as plot development, dialogue, metaphor, theme, and characterization. CMs rely on fact and on the author's memory. Some aspects of our lives are matters of verifiable written or photographic (or video) record: a child's or parent's birth date, the year in which we acquired our beloved pet, the recipe for Aunt Lou's best ever chocolate pie eaten at every Thanksgiving dinner, or the marginal notes our brother the minister wrote in his Bible. Other aspects of our lives are grounded in memories and perceptions. Did my sister really *always* take the last piece of chicken from the dinner platter? Did my father fail to show up for any of my high school volleyball games? One member of the family may recall a set of events or experience emotions triggered by a family story in ways not shared by others in the family, by close friends, or by other important people. CM authors use facts when they can; but they also, of necessity, create probable details related to life events to fill gaps in the storyline. CMs also rely on memory, and memory is fallible. The details that CM authors use, however, must ring true to the people, times, and facts of their lives. This distinction might be characterized by the difference between *Truth* and *truth*. *Truth* is verifiable fact, while an individual's memories, emotions, relationships, and associations color *truth*. It is *True* my sister was born in 1982; it is my perception— my individual *truth*—that she instantly became the favorite child, a perception she might dispute even though I may recall details that support my opinion. CM, then, is a highly personalized, readable, entertaining, and engrossing genre for a variety of reasons.

Having thought through the possibilities of CM, my inquiry focused next on the extent to which avid fiction readers like Danielle and her girlfriends would respond to CM. Would they be at all interested? Would they personalize nonfiction with the same energy they devoted to fiction? Would they find relevance in CM? Would they even like the genre and choose to read it? And, finally, would they write about their own lives in ways similar to those they used when extending the fiction they read? If so, what import would their interactions hold? All of these questions helped guide me as I worked with Danielle and her friends.

Composing a Life

For many devoted readers, interactions with texts shape and help direct thinking, opinions, and ways of knowing. What we learn and the emotions triggered from reading contribute to who we are and who we become as sensate beings. In effect, our engagement with texts helps us compose our lives, much as Danielle and her friends compose fiction. The phrase *composing a life* is adapted from Mary Bateson (1989; 2010) and is grounded in early research into what Belenky et al. (1986) termed women's *ways of knowing*. This seminal work suggests that women are relational in their ways of viewing the world, solving problems, and seeking happiness. Women construct their realities, in part, by considering how they are connected to others and the quality of the relationships in their lives. Though Danielle and her friends would not recount their activities and friendships in such terms, their emphasis on connectedness is evident in how they spend their time, what they deem important, and how they speak and write about their current experiences and their futures.

The notion of actively composing a life contrasts with traditional views of both females and reading. Thankfully, literacy research and pop culture opinions about literacy-related activities have evolved significantly during the last several decades. Traditionally, females are depicted as reading more frequently and as writing more texts (letters, poems, short stories) than are males, especially in traditional genres. One needs to look no further than to a classic work such as *Little Women* for a socio-cultural, psychological tableau of how girls are to fill their lives properly. As period pieces, novels like Alcott's both reflect and promote many of the race, class, and gender biases common to the time in which the texts were written. For decades, gendered biases led many to conclude that females—as the quieter, less active gender—engaged in reading because it was a solitary, quiet, and unobtrusive activity. In contrast, males were depicted as engaged in *action*—working at jobs outside the home, chopping wood, and mowing the lawn—which reading clearly was not. Currently, a good deal of research debunks the notion that reading and writing are isolated, solitary activities. Constructivists conceive of all knowledge as being actively built by the individual. This is a theoretical stance that has been applied successfully to reading and has transformed notions of reading from a passive pursuit to one of engaged activity. Much of what I noted in my study supports this theory.

Danielle and her friends most assuredly view reading and writing as action and as social and artistic engagement. Most of Danielle's group eschewed conventional social networks as being too static. The girls thrive on active, real-time feedback and response. Most will easily and quickly lose themselves in their self-selected reading and writing. Whether they are online, reading conventional books, or writing with physical pens on physical papers, Danielle and her friends engage with and reflect upon their reading. They internalize, commit to memory, and construct plotlines and characters related to their reading. They are *active readers*, making connections among what they read, write, and experience in their lives. These girls are wired in, connected, intellectually agile, and exceptionally literate young adults. They see their creative and social time as a method of sorting their emotions, discussing their lived experiences, and venturing into future possibilities. Importantly, they intersect with technology, literacy, and social connectedness to build their realities. They are *composing their lives* on numerous levels even as they live them. Still, my question remained: Would the girls respond to and engage with nonfiction, specifically with Contemporary Memoirs (CMs), especially those written for young adults this age, as they did with fiction?

Transitioning to Contemporary Memoir (CM)

Before asking the girls to read any CMs, I engaged them first in remembering key events, people, and places from their childhoods. The technique involves inter-twining reading, reflecting, talking, and writing in order to explore memory, recall details, and reflect upon significance. As I have detailed elsewhere (Kirby and Kirby 2007), beginning with teen writers' lived experiences is crucial throughout the processes of developing abilities as readers and writers. When young adults are encouraged to remember *meaningful moments*, they both recall and re-imagine their experiences. This cognitive, reflective work is especially vital to the processes that support young adults as writers, helping them create authentic texts and engaging them in writing they are committed to revising.

Several beginning explorations of people and events have been especially successful for me when working with young adults as they start writing about their lives. I usually begin by having them write about their names, calling this writing simply the "Name Piece." Exploring what they know about their names combines a bit of research into the meaning of their names, how they are connected to their families and cultures through their names, and how their names have afforded them opportunities and, perhaps, some embarrassments. Samantha, for example, wrote about the confusion caused on a social network when she created a profile using only her nickname, Sam. Sam posted a picture of herself with her younger brother, and then posted in her status information that she had a boyfriend. Much confusion ensued. Fortunately, Sam was able to bring humor to her recounting of the trails of misunderstandings that resulted from her nickname and social networking choices. Questions about names that I used with the girls in the study to prompt exploration included ones like the following:

- Who named you?
- How does your name connect you to your family?
- Are you named after an aunt, grandmother, or mother's best friend?
- What does your name mean in English and/or other languages?
- What other names did you almost have?
- What other names have you wished you had?

After considering the questions, the girls created columns for each of their names: first, middle, last, and nicknames. In each column they jotted details they knew about their names, including memories like the one from Samantha, or responses to the questions. After about ten minutes, I asked the girls to talk about their jottings. To begin the discussion and to model the technique of recalling specific details to enhance writing, I began by relating to the girls my remembrance of discovering that "aurora" means "dawn," and then of wanting to change my name to "Aurora" when I was in third grade. During the discussion that followed, the girls recalled book characters with that name as well as some of the names they once fancied. They speculated about how long I might have continued as Aurora rather than Dawn, had I changed my name.

After this initial recalling, writing, and talking activity, we read a "Name Piece" from a young adult's point of view, "My Name" in Sandra Cisneros' *The House on Mango Street* (1984), a novel frequently taught in secondary schools and one which all of the girls had read. Though not a CM, Cisneros' novel is highly autobiographical and serves as a transitional text between fiction and CM. Among the techniques Cisneros uses in this piece are metaphor, cultural references, supposition, detail, and showing rather than telling. With this professional author's writing and our previous thinking, talking, and remembering at the forefront, all the girls were able to write about their names. I encouraged them to go beyond exposition and surface meanings associated with their names, asking that they also attach personal meaning, emotion, and significance to their names (or to some part of their names). I wanted them to write about those more profound associations not only as a way of encouraging deeper reflection, but also as a way of drawing the reader into their writing. The girls were all able to relate some kind of incident involving their names; one wrote about the relative after whom she was named, another wrote about a relative involved in her name selection, and one wrote about the difficulty caused by being known by her middle name.

After composing an initial draft of these pieces, we continued talking about names, asking questions about missing details in the girls' texts, and reflecting on what emotions were associated with their names. Danielle drafted both a prose passage about her name and a poem about her personality, ultimately combining them to produce a mixed-genre piece:

> My mother liked the name from the beginning, books she used to read by an author named Danielle Steele accounting for some of her attraction to the name, I guess. She also married my dad, Dan, and liked the idea of having my name connect me to both of them. She tried out Dani as a name in her head but decided it was too confusing to have a male Dan and a female Dani in the same house. She wanted a name that was feminine. Danielle was a natural. I like Dani. It sounds sophisticated and a little bit tough. I am neither of those things. Maybe a name like Dani could have helped me be bolder. More out there. What am I?
>
> D is for dogged, the only way I get through math
> A is for amused, what I try to be
> N is for nutty, which I think is a positive trait
> I is for I, myself, me, alone
> E is for effervescent, a vocabulary word from sixth grade that makes me
>   laugh when I think of literally bubbly people
> L is for lonely, which I am sometimes as an only child
> L is redundant, another one in the same name, but who needs to be
>   doubly lonely?
>
> E is for extra, the extra person, the one with only I, not the one who fits in. Danielle is who I am. I am not a Dani. I fit with my dad and my mother. I fit with my friends. And maybe that's enough. For now. But one day, maybe I'll wear a glittery cape and a sassy red dress, get a Jennifer Goodwin short haircut, and become a Dani to be reckoned with.

This piece of writing certainly reveals insights about Danielle, her doubts and hopes, and her perception of her social status. By trying out a name that she might have liked, she is using Cisneros' technique, one that we discussed as being funny and almost sad simultaneously. Her writing captures the angst of girls her age and the bittersweet state of being poised between self-doubt and self-knowledge. The girls continued writing about their names for the next few weeks, revising and adding to their first drafts, until each had a name piece that she was proud to share with the group. Our initial foray into these remembering, reading, and writing processes established the routines that we then used for a number of additional explorations.

When working with the girls to help them craft individual memoir pieces, I guided them through linked remembering, reading, and writing processes, helping them recall significant aspects of their lives. Though perhaps not the stuff of fame and fortune, everyone has events and emotions to share with an audience and to which an audience may relate. The processes of exploring memories' significance and import not only helped these girls craft meaningful pieces of writing, but also allowed them to reveal and understand much more about themselves and the forces shaping them. We discussed that, because they are still in high school, more events and people will continue to inform who they become as adults. Key to their maturation process is their awareness and renewed discovery of who they are and who they have the potential to become.

Additional Writing Techniques

In addition to adding details that convey not only time and place but also emotion and relationships, several other composing techniques contributed to the girls' growth as thinkers and writers. We continued using the pattern of talking, writing, and reading in recursive ways to help craft written pieces. One technique involved reading dialogue carefully both to study its purpose within the overall piece and to understand what it taught us about writing realistic dialogue—a task much more difficult than the girls thought it would be. Dialogue was then incorporated into the pieces the girls were writing to help reveal character, mood, opinion, and other details as their narratives of lived experiences developed.

A favorite technique of the girls that we discussed is that of writing about a past event as though it is occurring in the present time. This technique, which I call a Snapshot Piece, helps draw the reader into the piece of writing, but it can also be used to enhance emotion. We discussed ways to use various sentence lengths to help pace the reader through a series of events that the writer is relating. Another strategy we used was sentence combining, especially important in avoiding unwanted choppiness. Using strong verbs with few adverbs (i.e., "sauntered" rather than "walked slowly") and other crafting techniques helped the girls revise their pieces to reflect memories, voices, emotions, and meanings.

A good example of how the girls applied what they were learning to the processes of reading and writing CM came when Courtney remembered with great delight her grandmother and the treats that emerged from her grandmother's oven. She felt close to her grandmother, confided in her, and tried to understand the wisdom contained in her loving advice. These were emotions and details Courtney discussed with the group as she reminisced about spending two weeks each summer with her grandparents in their small, yet comfortable, house. However, when she started to write about one of her clearest memories from these special times, a key portion of her first draft read simply: "I went into the kitchen and saw tears on my grandmother's face. She said she was fine, but I didn't believe her. She was thinking about my mother and my uncle again, and I knew she was sad." Together, we jotted details about the room, the conversation that must have occurred, and the likelihood that something was baking in the oven. We worked with verb tense and sentence variety. We discussed how to reveal the cause of the crying and the effect it had on her. After much effort, Courtney revised her original three sentences to produce the following:

> I am walking into my grandmother's yellow and blue kitchen. A ray of early morning sunlight sparkles the yellow paint on the walls and silvers the blue cabinets. It is a warm kitchen, warm from the cookies in the oven and warm with love. My grandmother, a trim woman as neat as her kitchen after she cleans up the utensils and flour from baking sugar cookies, sits at the wooden table that once was a door to her childhood home. "Mornin', Grandma. What's up?"
>
> My grandma's left hand brushes something away from her right cheek. I hear a sniff. She says, "Your favorite cookies are in the oven, ready in five minutes." She still faces the wall, not yet turning to face me. Her voice sounds hoarse as if someone is closing their hand over her throat.
>
> "Grandma? Is something wrong?" I cross the kitchen and stand behind her. I place my hand on her shoulder. She pats my hand and stands up, turning to me. "Some mornings like this, I remember your mother and can't believe how quickly time passes. Seems that she was your age just yesterday. And now we hardly speak. I can't help but wonder why she still blames me for her brother's hardships." She pauses before almost whispering, "Grudges don't do a body any good." Grandma talks that way sometimes, old-fashioned, sad, trying to make everything right even when she knows she can't.

Courtney clearly garnered more detail into her writing and actually created a scene, not just a few vague sentences, from her memory. She added detail, created and conveyed emotion, wrote in the present tense, and used conversation to enliven her writing. It is neither a perfect nor an error-free piece of writing, but her commitment to it and to the meaning of the scene is clear in her extensive revision efforts.

Reading Contemporary Memoirs

After grounding our preliminary work in personal details, narrative stance, a store of effective writing techniques, and multiple readings and writings, the group was ready to move into reading CMs written for and appealing to young adults. CMs are numerous and fill bookstore shelves. Finding CMs for young adults, however, can be more challenging. Though more are written each year, the percentage of CMs for young adults is small when compared to the overall number of CM titles. Still, the range of topics addressed in CMs for young adults is extensive. Young adults who want to read about authors of favorite childhood fiction will find CMs by Gary Paulsen, Lois Lowery, Jack Gantos, Beverly Cleary, Roald Dahl, Walter Dean Myers, and others. Personal involvement in historically significant events has spawned CMs by individuals such as Ishmael Beah, Rita la Fontaine de Clercq Zubli, and Melba Pattillo Beals. Those with special abilities and challenges have written CMs, including Daniel Tammet and Samantha Abeel. Addiction is the subject of CMs by Nic Sheff and Koren Zailckas, while Nathan L. Henry writes about his early criminal behavior and time in prison. This very short sampling of recent CMs indicates the variety of YA models with which teens may engage.

It is also clear that available CMs can be gritty, frank, and intentionally or unintentionally didactic. If curious about the effects of alcohol, for example, a teen need not become a drunk, but may instead have a vicarious experience by reading CMs by teen alcoholics, who, in a second CM, may relate their journey to recovery. Danielle and her friends read a variety of CMs that appealed to them personally. Though they did not enact role-plays as they did for the fiction they read, the girls discussed the books with enthusiasm, read with intensity, and reached into their own memories to explore and reflect on experiences. Reading first-hand accounts of past cultural practices like foot binding sometimes surprised the girls, the writing forming vivid images that they continued to call upon for their own CM expressions. Alexis, for example, was horrified by Li's account in *Snow Falling in Spring* (2008) of her grandmother's experience and the relatives who would endorse what seemed to be a brutal act:

> "This will hurt ... but after a while, the pain will go away." Looking from her auntie to her *baba*, who stood tensely watching, Lao Lao [Li's grandmother] did not know what to say. Suddenly, Auntie reached out and bent Lao Lao's toes under, one after another, hard, and started to wrap the linen bandage around Lao Lao's tiny foot, each round of cloth tighter than the last.
>
> The pain came so fast and was so sharp that Lao Lao burst into tears. Tearing the cloth loose from her foot ... she ran out of the house. ... She hid in a corner of their courtyard, sobbing. [Baba] could not bear to watch his daughter suffer, and the short-lived foot-binding experiment ended. As Lao Lao grew older, her natural beauty and her natural feet surprised people equally. Her father accepted this with good humor, dubbing her feet *tianzu* (heavenly feet). (25)

Alexis responded to this CM excerpt by writing about her own mother and a particularly difficult episode in their relationship:

> I have not always been a "good girl." In eighth grade, I liked to sneak out of my house at night and meet my friends on the corner. The older kids drive and smoke while us younger ones giggle and swear to show we're cool with what we're doing. After one particular night out, I crawled into my open window to find my mother sitting on my bed. Damn. Caught. Tried. Crucified. I felt no pain. She didn't hit me or yell at me. She talked. And talked. Did I know what could happen to me? Did I know how she worried? Did I know how lucky I was to live where and how we did? She was always *there*, always talking, always making a point, teaching me a "life lesson," as she called it. Except for those night time trips out of my window, my feet might as well have been bound for all the distance I could have from her.

Reading about foot binding clearly formed a strong emotional and metaphoric image in Alexis' mind that she then applied in her writing to describe some of her feelings about her mother. In conversations about this piece of writing, Alexis revealed how worried she was about being branded as a "bad kid" who would not behave. Taking honors classes and making straight As in all of them had not removed the stigma of her earlier actions:

> I never thought about how to describe my reactions and what I was thinking except to bad-mouth my mother and swear sometimes. But the foot binding thing. That really stuck with me and expressed my feelings of being hobbled like a horse and tied to my family.

The power of metaphor became very real to Alexis as she read CMs and wrote about her experiences.

For Summer, the technique of slowing down time through the use of minute detail became quite influential in her writing and thinking. One of the CM excerpts that resonated for her is found in Irene Opdyke's account of trying to protect Jews during the Holocaust. Opdyke (1999) writes:

> As if through a fog, I noticed a sound from the hallway, and before I could speak, the kitchen door swung open and the [German] major came in.
>
> There are these moments before calamity strikes—before the dropped crystal shatters on the floor, before the car's fender smashes against the racing dog, before the drunken man's hand strikes the child's face—when time stretches out and each second is wrapped in silence.
>
> And then the world crashes.

Summer noted the techniques used by the author to create the effect of slow motion: creating specific, familiar images of motion; repeating the word "before" to cause the reader to replay the motion before, during, and after its occurrence in real time; and using the final one-sentence paragraph to return our minds to the action in motion and its conclusion. She responded that, after reading this CM excerpt, she replayed vivid past experiences in her mind in slow motion to capture the detail needed to make an impact with the reader:

> I see myself with my dog, running, foot leaving the pavement, thigh and calf at right angles for a split second, foot hitting the pavement, and the entire sequence repeating itself. Trying to write that way, to think about what is happening first, second and third, helps me create more concrete images in my fiction and in my memories.

Summer further relates: "I feel like a director shooting a movie. I know what I want to see, what I want the actors to do, and it's my job to get it on film—even if it's the film playing in my mind." Finally, she concludes: "I feel good about being able to create pictures in my mind and in the reader's mind. It helps me write better and describe almost everything more richly." These comments echoed activities the girls carried out in their role-plays based on fiction readings. Clearly, the writers' techniques the girls studied, discussed, and tried produced highly involved, positive outcomes in their writing of fiction and of CM.

Affecting Girls' Self-Knowledge through Contemporary Memoir (CM)

The reading and writing, talking and reflecting experiences outlined here had positive influences on these girls' writing abilities, giving them techniques to improve and enhance any type of writing they produced. The crossover nature of creative nonfiction, of which CM is a part, allowed the girls to understand that good writing in any genre shares certain characteristics; that they, as writers, have the ability to analyze and use these distinctive techniques to enhance personally written pieces of any genre; and that reflecting on lived experiences helps one understand the self and who that self is more fully becoming. Through their understandings, the girls experienced increased confidence, realization of agency, self-efficacy, and the knowledge that they could—and no doubt would—use their cognitive and literate abilities to compose meaningful life events and attitudes.

In a final discussion, the girls verbalized some of their insights. Summer said, "I think I have it bad sometimes, and I get really mad at my parents for being snoopy; but they love me and are trying hard to raise me right. I'm lucky." Alexis noted, "I *have* changed how I act, and my parents are trying to trust me more. I think I can get this thing right. I think I can please them *and* be the person *I* want to be, too." Danielle mentioned liking the family connections her name gives her and planning to pass a similar legacy on to her own children some day. Courtney gained philosophical insights about some of the tensions in her family dynamics and clarity about their history, realizing fully that events were in motion well before she was even born. Perhaps Danielle said it best:

I love writing, and I read constantly. Without a book in my hands or a story in my head, I feel lost. But now I know the story is and should be mine, not just some fictional character's. And I know I can create my own endings, at least some of the time.

CM revealed to these girls their experiences and reactions to their experiences. By working with this genre, the girls saw links between reading and writing fiction and nonfiction and found a new interest in reading creative nonfiction such as CM.

Connecting with Diverse Teens

Teens spend much of their young lives in school. Teachers lecture, lead discussions, allocate assignments, administer assessments, and try to motivate students' learning. High-stakes tests and the recent move toward a common national curriculum affect funding for schools and districts. These trends also directly affect what is taught and the instructional methods and materials teachers are allowed and willing to use. These are some very real limitations of school contexts, limitations that do not favor curricular innovation and student motivation. Such motivation works best, of course, when it is intrinsic; but how do we create interest in school and learning for all students?

At least part of the response lies in academic engagement. For both teachers and teens, realizing that literacy engagement can be crafted, that it benefits from reflection, and that it is highly useful beyond the school context is vital for promoting girls' academic and life successes. Throughout my work with CM, I have studied girls of differing race and socio-economic status, girls who are at-risk rather than highly successful in school, girls from single- and dual-parent homes, and girls with varying sexual orientations. For some girls, like those in this study, engagement may be strengthened by social uses of technology and by extending reading through role-play and image-rich thinking. For others, just talking about their lives is a key motivator. A teen's favorite topic is reportedly "me." One of the most alluring features of CM is that the young adult author is the expert on her life. A powerful or influential figure—friend, parent, or teacher—does not have the exact personal experiences and perceptions needed to make CM live on the page as do the teen authors writing it. These are precisely the types of inspiration and learning that promote increased literacy for all girls.

A significant point is that when girls interact with each other and with CM, their sense of agency increases. The self-knowledge that girls gain from reading and writing CM empowers them to understand that they are creating their experiences, values, and perceptions not only through their actions, but also through the ways in which they reflect upon their actions. Reading and writing CM, therefore, provide positive, concrete, and absorbing ways to improve girls' literacy, which in turn leads to increased opportunities for success in other areas of their lives. Most importantly, by working with CM, girls have a distinct opportunity to notice myriad ways in which they are figuratively and literally composing their lives.

Acknowledgments

I want to thank the real teens behind these case studies. All of the names are pseu-donyms, used because none of the teens wished to be identified by first and last names. All writings from the girls who agreed to share them appear without correction.

Works Cited

Bateson, Mary C. *Composing a Life*. New York: Grove/Atlantic Press, 1989. Print.
——*Composing a Further Life: The Age of Active Wisdom*. New York: Grove Press, 2010. Print.
Belenky, Mary, Blythe Clinchy, Nancy Goldberger, and Jill Tarule. *Women's Ways of Knowing: The Development of Self, Voice, and Mind*. New York: Basic Books, 1986. Print.
Cisneros, Sandra. *The House on Mango Street*. Logan, IA: Perfection Learning, 1984. Print.
Kirby, Dawn L. and Dan Kirby. *New Directions in Memoir: A Studio Classroom Approach*. Portsmouth, NH: Heinemann, 2007. Print.
Li, Moying. *Snow Falling in Spring: Coming of Age in China during the Cultural Revolution*. New York: Farrar, Straus and Giroux, 2008. Print.
Opdyke, Irene Gut, with Jennifer Armstrong. *In My Hands: Memories of a Holocaust Rescuer*. New York: Random House, 1999. Print.

PART III

Popular Culture, Technology, and the New Media

7

GIRLHOOD, AGENCY, AND POP CULTURE LITERACY

The *Twilight* Saga as Exemplar

Katie Kapurch

Introduction

Often clad in a black t-shirt featuring the image of a brooding cinematic Edward Cullen, twelve-year-old Liza is known as "thetwilightreader" on YouTube, a popular video streaming website. She usually films herself speaking to a camera amid the backdrop of her cluttered bedroom, which is decked out in posters and homemade artwork honoring the Young Adult (YA) *Twilight* Saga, a popular vampire romance by Stephenie Meyer. Over the course of a year (2009–10), Liza directed, edited, and posted more than eighty videos on her personal YouTube channel, which began as a project to celebrate the novels, characters, films, songs, and actors associated with the *Twilight* phenomenon. In her "10 Reasons Why I Love Twilight" video, Liza enumerates factors that led to her fascination:

> Number Seven. It's AD-DIC-TING! It really is, I mean really, okay, like the first time I read *Twilight*, I wasn't—I knew I'd probably like it but I wasn't quite sure that I'd get *that* into it, so I didn't buy the book. I just borrowed it from my teacher. (I own it now. [chuckles knowingly] Second time I'm going to read it.) But, like, when I first got the book, my Language Arts teacher came into my Social Studies class, handed it to me real quick and said, "Don't lose it" (because I lose things all the time) and then walked out the door. I read the first sentence: "I"—[begins to mime the action, but runs back to her unmade daybed for the book, which she opens] "I'd never given much thought to how I would die—though I'd had reason enough in the last few months—but even if I had, I would not have imagined it like this." [closes the book, then reconsiders, giving the novel a double take] That's a run-on sentence, but oh well. [shrugs before looking intently into the

camera] I was already addicted to it. I didn't want to go to PE class. I wanted to go home and lie on my couch and read the rest. But [sighing] really, it's addicting. If you haven't read it—warning: it's going to be like your "own personal brand of heroin." HAHAHA. Ahhhhh, you need to see the movie.

Ending on an allusion to vampire Edward's characterization of girl protagonist Bella Swan, Liza goes on to explain how another novel in the Saga became a welcome, but forbidden, distraction from her science class.

Liza's story provides a thought-provoking starting point when thinking about girls, popular culture, and the role of English teachers. Acknowledging her initial skepticism, Liza provides anecdotal evidence of the importance of her English teacher's endorsement, which has a direct influence on Liza's literacy and, subsequently, her sense of belonging to what Frank Smith in *The Book of Learning and Forgetting* calls a "literacy club" (25). Liza reveals how *Twilight* inspired her to read and think critically about reading, as evidenced by her textual allusions and commentary about Meyer's opening sentence. This particular video also suggests how contemporary novels and their cinematic counterparts offer girls a pleasurable escape from the daily demands of adolescence through a medium teachers encourage, written text. Other videos on Liza's channel disclose her self-conscious tendencies while illustrating how *Twilight* became an avenue to friendships with other girls (both at school and online), encouraging her to embrace her self-consciousness. Liza chooses media production to build connections, channel her creative energy, and gain confidence, a trend common, as I will show, among other girls as well.

In responding through "girl-made media" (Kearney, *Girls*) to a phenomenally popular text featuring an adolescent female protagonist, Liza's example embodies a contemporary moment concerning girls in twenty-first century Western popular culture. This moment, as feminist scholars observe, is *in part* a continuation of conspicuous mass-mediated efforts to position girls as desirable consumers, an ideological disposition whereby consumerism is the primary means to female empowerment (Kearney, "Coalescing" 14; Durham 28–29; Griffin). On top of that, the incorporation of feminist themes in mass media, coupled with a discursive emphasis on the female body as a site of contest (i.e., "Girl Power" rhetoric), mean that ostensibly empowered female adolescent protagonists are still bound by narratives that ultimately favor hegemony (Durham; Harris; Griffin; Saxton xxi). In other words, as Durham argues, especially works that tend toward the supernatural (such as *Buffy the Vampire Slayer*) reflect a version of female empowerment that is constrained by ideologies that privilege whiteness, blondness, thinness, and heterosexuality, "all in the interests of capital" (3). Those familiar with the history of texts directed at girls recognize the pattern and contradictions inherent in these narratives. For example, it remains unclear for some even today if the groundbreaking Nancy Drew of the 1930s was a feminist role model or only a modern day daughter of patriarchy.

While the contradictory representations of empowered girlhood are well documented, such findings provide only part of the picture of girl culture, which Liza's circumstance proves. As Sherrie A. Inness notes: "It is important to consider the culture that girls themselves create as active producers and shapers of their realities as well as the culture that is created and shaped by adults and then marketed to girls, who, in their turn, shape market-place commodities in ways that might or might not have been intended by their adult creators" (4). With increased visibility through online spaces (Kearney, "Productive" 137; Mazzarella), girls agentially position themselves as producers as they actively engage pop culture, often disrupting and blending the previously discrete boundaries between various forms of media (literature, film, and music). Liza as "thetwilightreader" is just one example of a girl reader and fan who complicates the consumer/producer binary through online media production as she addresses *Twilight*, a phenomenon that has inspired other examples of girl-made media like Liza's.

Using the *Twilight* Saga as a representative text, my chapter first explores contradictory depictions of female adolescent agency, particularly in the context of intimate relationships, in popular culture. Noting how Bella's conflicts speak to adolescent girlhood, I suggest *Twilight* addresses tensions consistent with other well-known depictions of "real life" coming-of-age girls and young women; these connections may help teachers appeal to girls in the English classroom. Following this premise, I argue mass-mediated texts function as agential opportunities for girls to create meaning, particularly through artistic works distributed online. These conclusions not only provide insight into the appeal of contemporary works (for example the *Twilight* Saga), which inspire critical and creative reflection among girls, but also suggest why popular culture should be harnessed to engage girls in the English classroom.

"He dazzled my eyes": Contradictory Representations of Female Agency

In *Twilight*, a first-person narrator, seventeen-year-old Bella, recounts the story of her move to the "small" and "inconsequential town" (3) of Forks, Washington, to live with her father, Charlie. Despite the relative blandness of the place, Bella is captivated by a brooding outsider, Edward, whose mysterious nature drives the girl's curiosity. When she learns about his monstrous condition of vampirism, Bella's romantic affection for Edward, who belongs to a coven with a moral conscience and whose skin sparkles in the sunlight, is only strengthened—even though Edward admits to thirsting hungrily for her blood.

The rest of *Twilight* and the subsequent Saga novels revel in the life-and-death intrigue that comes with a teenage girl's entanglement with the supernatural. Bella's life is in jeopardy when evil vampires threaten Forks, and her romantic involvement with Edward is complicated by the always-looming danger of his bite, thus prohibiting the sexual experimentation for which Bella yearns. On top of this, a shape-shifting werewolf, Jacob, competes with Edward not only as a sworn supernatural foe, but also as a romantic rival. The contradictory representations of Bella's sexual agency are epitomized by these romantic conflicts, especially since Bella's desires are thwarted by her relative lack of say-so when it comes to physical intimacy with Edward, who has strict rules about what constitutes "safe" levels of erotic closeness. As Carrie Anne Platt notes:

> The prevalence of sexual desire—and the constant policing of this desire— reflect cultural contradictions surrounding sex in American culture. This tension is particularly acute for the YA audience, who has come of age in an era of abstinence-only sex education and public declarations of sexual purity, juxtaposed against an increasingly sexualized media culture. (84)

Again, an historical look at this phenomenon, as seen in scholarship such as Mary E. Odem's *Delinquent Daughters: Protecting and Policing Adolescent Female Sexuality in the United States, 1885–1920* (1995), helps us understand the public reaction to any appeal of popular culture for girls.

To say, however, that Bella Swan is a character without agency would be a mischaracterization. From the beginning of the series, part of Bella's draw is her maturity, evidenced through the responsibility she assumes for her divorced parents. Prior to relocating to Forks, Bella's youth was spent parenting her "loving, erratic, hare-brained mother" (*Twilight* 4). Once she moves in with her well meaning, but emotionally distant father, Charlie, Bella continues to "parent" but in a different way; she shops for groceries, does laundry, and cooks. This Cinderella-scenario provides an appealing and familiar narrative; it follows that readers will root for the beautiful prince, Edward, to provide a distraction from the lackluster domesticity of Bella's everyday life. As an "orphan" of sorts, Bella is attracted to Edward *in part* because of his devotion to her since she clearly has grown up without such dedicated attention.

In relation to sexuality, however, the implication of female desire as dangerous is an ongoing motif, an observation also made by Platt's scholarly critique. Bella's amorous advances create a scenario in which Edward could kill her; as he decrees in *Twilight*, "'I can never, never afford to lose any kind of control when I'm with you'" (310). Yet, this does not hinder Bella from actively desiring Edward, particularly through descriptions of his allure: "His eyes were wild, his jaw clenched in acute restraint, yet he didn't lapse from his perfect articulation. He held my face just inches from his. He dazzled my eyes" (282). Bella's expressed desire for Edward and eroticized appreciation of particular parts of his body are historically consistent with the kind of sexual awakenings available in popular YA novels—from Judy Blume's *Forever* (1975) to the vastly different *Angus, Thongs and Full-Frontal Snogging* (1999) by Louise Rennison.

Depictions of a heroine's intense longing also align Bella with another well-known female narrator, one who loves a similarly moody man, Edward Rochester, a connection I have developed elsewhere in relation to shared melodramatic impulses (Kapurch). Before the advent of texts written specifically for girls, popular culture also presented itself to young women in texts now considered classics. In Charlotte Brontë's coming-of-age novel *Jane Eyre* (1847), Jane's yearnings are presented like Bella's—passionate but frequently thwarted. Justifying *Jane Eyre*'s lasting appeal, Sandra M. Gilbert suggests:

> That *Jane Eyre* introduced audiences to the 'wild declarations' and egalitarian strivings of an unprecedentedly passionate heroine certainly explains why the novel has always had a special appeal for women, who tend to identify—and want to identify—with this compelling narrator's powerful voice. (357)

Gilbert's astute insight into Jane's relatability may help to explain the current popularity of texts like *Twilight*, associated not only with *Jane Eyre* but also Emily Brontë's *Wuthering Heights*, Bella's preferred reading material within the series itself (see *Eclipse*). Recognizing popular works' connections to now-canonical literature enriches the potential for the English classroom to speak to girls' everyday lives.

Complicating Meyer's representation of Bella's sexual agency is the reader's exclusive access to Bella's personal yearnings. While her blood is the most appealing Edward has ever sensed, her thoughts are inexplicably inaccessible to him, even though telepathy is his particular vampire strength. As a result, Bella actually does have the capacity to deny Edward mental penetration—as he denies her physical intimacy. Increasingly, Edward is charged with resisting Bella's growing physical desire until they reach what might be considered an unsettling bargain. At the beginning of the last novel in the Saga, *Breaking Dawn*, Bella explains:

> Edward and I were together, and I'd fulfilled my side of our compromise perfectly. I'd married him. That was the big one. ... Now it was his turn. Before he turned me into a vampire—his big compromise—he had one other stipulation to make good on. ... I wanted a real honeymoon with Edward. And, despite the danger he feared this would put me in, he'd agreed to try. (21–22)

Though Bella lacks sexual agency in her relationship with Edward throughout the series, this tension is localized in *Breaking Dawn*. To overcome her anxiety about the wedding, Bella focuses singularly on Edward and the honeymoon, her "happy place" (22), which holds the promise of the erotic moment she desires. Yet, Bella's sexual initiation is characterized by sex that ravages her body so severely that she wakes up with terrible bruises to a brooding husband in a broken bed. Consistent with her typical self-doubt, a "product of a lifetime of insecurities" (87), Bella thinks Edward is angry because of *her* performance, but later learns Edward's anger is directed toward himself. Despite Edward's initial refusal, the couple manage to consummate their marriage again with less bruising and bed-breaking because

Edward learns to further control his strength. Understanding these representations of physical intimacy begs a consideration of what constitutes female agency, especially in adolescence. Recognizing and responding to such thought-provoking contradictions in mass media, including popular cinematic adaptations of literature like the *Twilight* Saga, are avenues to fostering students' critical relationships with texts and exploring questions of consequence to them.

What might constitute female agency in the *Twilight* Saga as an exemplar of contemporary popular culture? Some would argue that Bella's decision to become a vampire gives her many things she desires, not the least of which is achieving the physical intimacy with Edward for which she has longed. And while feminist-leaning editorials criticize Bella for her damsel-in-distress moments (Johnson; Fralic), the narrator does recognize the need for equality from the beginning of the Saga:

> "I'll be the first to admit that I have no experience with relationships. … But it just seems logical … a man and woman have to be somewhat equal … as in, one of them can't always be swooping in and saving the other one. They have to save each other *equally*." (*Twilight* 473–74)

Interestingly, that kind of thinking is consistent with the kind of equality for which Jane Eyre hungers and that she and Rochester ultimately achieve at the end of Brontë's novel.

Bella's distaste for decoration and expensive goods as well as her discomfort with the spotlight—expressed plainly through her narration to the reader—are relatable attributes that may also signify agential qualities in the female protagonist. She only reluctantly takes the showy car Edward offers to protect her, after consistently refusing the splendid gifts and conveniences with which he has tirelessly attempted to shower her throughout the series. She does not really want the extravagance associated with the wedding upon which Edward's sister, Alice, insists. In both cases, however, she does recognize the need for compromise, a quality that should not render her devoid of agency. Again, Bella resembles Jane Eyre, who tries to go unnoticed in the company of Thornfield Estates' upper-class visitors and whose sensibility makes her later decline Rochester's efforts to inundate her wardrobe with lavish bridal clothes, and insist instead upon the compromise of a "lilac gingham" (269).

Bella's remarks about exterior luxuries being inconsistent with her true personality additionally resemble sentiments expressed in Louisa May Alcott's *Little Women*: "I'm not Meg tonight, I'm 'a doll' who does all sorts of crazy things. Tomorrow I shall put away my 'fuss and feathers' and be desperately good again" (89). In this way, Bella is much more like nineteenth century heroines than recent predecessors, like Buffy (the vampire slayer) Summers, who proclaims: "I just want to get my life back, you know, do normal stuff … date and shop and hang out and go to school and save the world from unspeakable demons. You know, I wanna do girlie stuff!" ("Faith, Hope, and Trick"). Bella's rejection of material consumption speaks to a rejection of contemporary discourses in popular culture that construct girls as avid and voracious consumers. This understanding advances an interpretation of Bella's agency: through her resistance to material luxuries, Bella subtly resists dominant culture's mandates that consumerism equals female empowerment, so often the ideological imperative levied at girls today.

Continuing Contradictions: Adapting Girlhood Curiosity for the Screen

The contradictory representations of female agency in the *Twilight* Saga are consistent with other mass-mediated representations of girlhood in popular culture, especially when it comes to sexuality and the female body. While girl characters are often empowered as sexual subjects, desiring (male) objects openly and actively, they are simultaneously sanctioned through narratives that encourage abstinence and virginity. Ruth O. Saxton describes this paradox in her study of girlhood in contemporary literature:

> In popular culture as well as literature we study in our college classrooms, the icons of the Girl are constantly being rewritten. The body of the young girl—whether athlete or potential Miss America—is the site of heated battles, not only among parents, teachers, coaches, but also those who would exploit her sexuality, lure her to internalize their fantasies and purchase their products. (xxi)

In fact, the first cinematic adaptation of Meyer's Saga, Catherine Hardwicke's *Twilight* (2008), adds to the paradoxical representations of female adolescence in popular culture by at once emphasizing Bella's sexual curiosity and then visualizing the resulting physical pain.

The cinematic portrayal of Bella's curious nature is mostly consistent with its literary predecessor. In both mediums, Meyer's protagonist is inquisitive and determined. Bella is able to sleuth out Edward's vampiric secret through a visit to an out-of-town bookstore, an Internet search, and the piecing together of clues, much like a modern-day Nancy Drew. However, while Hardwicke's film generally upholds this and other major plots originated by the novel, deleted scenes on the DVD offer a few significant revisions. In addition to shots that depict Bella dreaming about pulling Edward onto her bed and into a sensual embrace, one especially provocative deleted scene shows Edward biting Bella's finger. As the camera hovers above their faces, Edward presses Bella's body to his own. She suggests suddenly, "Do you want a taste?" and Edward responds huskily, "Yeah." Bella puts her finger in Edward's mouth, and he bites with rising intensity. As their breathing accelerates, Bella makes little gasps until she can no longer stand the pain. She smiles and puts her finger in her own mouth to soothe the ache while Edward responds, "Fragile, little human." Once the biting has subsided, the couple's breathing is still heavy and labored, as if the bite—both the acts of biting and being bitten—involves concerted effort. Despite the latter lines, which are available in Meyer's novel, such experimental biting would violate the literary Edward's vigilant mindfulness about physical intimacy and his chivalrous commitment to Bella's safety.

Although this scene is deleted from the film, the experimental intimacy still exists as part of the text of the DVD. Such cinematic visualization may also replicate the kind of alternate fantasies fans perform through fan fiction and role-playing activities. At first, one might interpret such a move as a kind of feminist intervention on the part of Hardwicke, reclaiming (hetero)sexual curiosity and experimentation in adolescent girlhood. Amy Bowles-Reyer notes that *Forever* accomplishes this kind of objective in 1975: "Blume participates in a feminist redefinition in public discourse of heterosexuality with an emphasis on female sexual pleasure" (34). Girls' active curiosity about physical intimacy with male partners, which even the literary Bella exemplifies, is a widely available message in popular culture. However, despite the seemingly radical and liberatory break with the literary text, the deleted scene still couples sexual experimentation with physical pain, a depiction that raises questions about anti-feminist messages in the *Twilight* phenomenon, and popular culture more generally. Such conclusions inspire the following questions: What do the differences between novel and film say about Meyer's and Hardwicke's interpretations of female adolescent sexuality? What do such differences say about contemporary girlhood in the U.S.? What are the reasons for the deleted scene failing to make the final cut of the film? Why is it important for girls to have a space to talk about the issues each of these texts present? Facilitated through comparative critiques of literary texts and their adaptations, these kinds of inquiries encourage critical engagement with not only contemporary works and messages found in popular culture, but also structures and conventions associated with more canonical texts, as the forthcoming analysis of genre reveals.

Why Genre Matters: Realism and Fantasy

After *Breaking Dawn*'s publication, Meyer defended her heroine against general accusations of being anti-feminist, explaining her "opinion" that "the foundation of feminism is this: being able to choose" ("Frequently"). While Meyer likely alludes to Bella's choice regarding her pregnancy, the representation of physical abuse as a justifiable consequence of sex arguably legitimizes relationship violence. Furthermore, Bella and Edward's sexual encounters result in her unplanned pregnancy, accompanied with the implied warning that protection (assumed vampire sterility) is not always foolproof. Moreover, a monstrous pregnancy and birthing experience, which produces a hybrid baby, are preferable to the termination option initially suggested by Edward when the contents of Bella's womb are unknown, a conclusion consistent with Meyer's conservative ideology (Platt 83). This cautionary tale adds to the kind of pervasive and contradictory messages about teen pregnancy in popular culture today, which Saxton summarizes: "Portrayed as a social failure if she procreates as a teenager, she is simultaneously taught that to be a mother is a mark of maturity and the passage to adulthood in society" (xxi). Through films like *Juno* (2008) and MTV's *16 and Pregnant* (2009–), the mass media today is full of stories about girls who experience the difficult, often painful consequences of failing to make sure sex is "safe" and who choose to see their pregnancy to completion.

Nevertheless, Meyer's plot does follow the mythic structure familiar to folklore and fantasy, in addition to nineteenth century works such as *Jane Eyre* and *Little Women* and even more current works like *The Hunger Games* trilogy. An inexperienced protagonist must undergo trials and tribulations to mature and develop as a person who is not only more confident in her abilities but also more sensitive and conscious of others, most often concluding with a marriage of equal partners. This is definitely the case with Bella; as the novel closes, she and Edward (now *both* stunningly beautiful and strong vampires) are set to enjoy marital, sexual bliss—for eternity. So, in this context, Bella's lack of confidence throughout the series makes sense; she is "not ready" for Edward—physically or mentally—since she yet has to complete a journey, which consists of a near-fatal pregnancy, an excruciatingly painful conversion from average girl to beautiful vampire, and participation in saving the morally good vampires from the bad vampires with her mind shield, a newly acquired vampire skill. Again, Bella's instrumental help and awareness of her own extraordinary abilities at the end of the series do support an interpretation that acknowledges her agency.

Despite this structural explanation, the limiting messages about human, female sexuality are indeed pervasive. Platt notes: "The overall ideological message is clear: to be young, female, and sexual is to court danger, destruction, and death" (80). Yet, the persistence of this problematic message may be explained through an analysis of the abrupt shifts in narrative and genre. At the beginning of *Breaking Dawn*, when the action is rooted in reality and when Bella is in her *human* form, her *human* desire is a threat to her safety, her *human* desire is immature, and it results in sex that is intertwined with physical harm and an unplanned pregnancy. Only after she enters the realm of the supernatural as a vampire (still in the confines of marriage) is her sexual desire appropriate and able to be explored, but at this point the novel takes on an entirely different tone than its three counterparts. Not only does the narrator's perspective temporarily shift from Bella to Jacob, but the genre also moves away from one of YA realism with profound supernatural elements (the real setting of Forks that happens to be home to a family of vampires) to a fantasy that loosely rests beside the real world—the characters are now set apart from the town, secluded in the Cullens' dwelling where a hybrid vampire–human baby ages in super-speed and Italian vampires parade into Northwest Washington seeking conflict. Instead of one dynamic character, in many ways the Saga offers two different Bellas—pre-vampire adolescent and post-vampire adult.

One may question whether these shifts in narrative and genre are due to an unresolved author; indeed, as the Saga goes on, the anticipation of a happy ending produces a problem Meyer is expected to resolve at the series' end. Bella's desire to turn vampire so she cannot age past Edward's age of seventeen might be better appreciated through acknowledging the context of a dominant culture that values youthfulness, especially for females. This consideration may explain, in part, why popular literature, film, and television are currently experiencing a marked increase in vampires and other paranormal subject matter (Kapurch). Offering more insight into an often-trivialized genre in her call for critical appreciation of the fantastic in adolescent literature, Elaine J. O'Quinn reveals: "in the haste to dismiss 'unrealistic' genres of books, we miss important understandings of adolescent thinking and identity construction" (51). O'Quinn further demonstrates how literary monsters, like the vampire, speak poignantly to lived experiences:

> The realization of their own mortality is important for all of the characters of these stories. Contrary to adult theory which would see teens as in denial of life's finitude, these YAL protagonists, vampires included, are able to recognize it with an emotional honesty that many adults fear. (54)

Given O'Quinn's insight, educators and scholars might further appreciate the profound seriousness of the circumstances in the *Twilight* Saga, especially the looming prospect of a sad farewell, which might be a realistic necessity if Bella is going to continue living in the real world and, say, pursue college and a career. Bella anxiously and fretfully fears this separation from Edward in addition to dying after aging past the vampire's visible youthful appearance.

Despite the shifting generic tendencies in the Saga, Meyer reports on her website that she knew the conclusion of the series "was going to revolve around a hybrid baby from the outset" ("Frequently"); the value of motherhood and female sexuality are furthermore linked. In fact, Meyer sees her work as "fantasy" and believes Bella's options and choices should be read in this context:

> this is not even realistic fiction, it's a fantasy with vampires and werewolves, so no one could ever make her exact choices. Bella chooses things differently than how I would … because she is a very different type of person than I am. Also, she's in a situation that none of us has ever been in, because she lives in a fantasy world. ("Frequently")

While it is true that literally no one could make Bella's "exact choices" because vampires and werewolves are supernatural, Meyer might be ignoring the important metaphorical implications of adolescent vampires and werewolves and the significance that many readers certainly glean from the text. As O'Quinn suggests:

> because they are in the midst of an evolving intellectual and emotional impression of the world, adolescents choose not to draw absolute lines between the conflicts that plague them and the conflicts that torment the characters they read about even if those conflicts are not necessarily their own and the characters exist in another realm. (50)

Furthermore, while *Breaking Dawn* plunges into fantasy, part of the series' previous appeal is its grounding in small town and high school reality—references to books and plays commonly read in English classes, activities like going to movies, hanging out in garages fixing motorcycles, major events such as a prom, birthdays, and graduation. Undoubtedly, everyday teenagers face choices related to major concepts with which the *Twilight* characters also wrestle: sex, romantic relationships, friendship, pregnancy, and commitment. Meyer has not created a completely separate fantasy world in which the action takes place, although her defense may explain the abrupt shift in narrative and why the character development seems rather disjointed.

The question thus remains—are the kinds of paradoxical messages about female agency inherent in popular culture, as exemplified by Bella and the contradictory messages about her agency, harmful to the girls who have made *Twilight* (and texts like it) so successful? In addition to Johnson and Fralic, Platt argues yes: "Bella is a troubling role model. Meyer has rendered her weak in both body and mind, giving her little to no agency when it comes to dealing with her physical attraction to Edward" (84). Although my analysis exemplifies why Bella's claims to agency are at times inconsistent, Platt's argument, first, ignores the agential aspects of Bella's intensity of feeling; even when she vacillates from conviction to indecisiveness and in the context of ideologically conservative choices, Bella does agentially negotiate intimate relationships.

Furthermore, while Platt does cite some studies that indicate girls seek information about sex and relationships from romance reading, Holly Virginia Blackford's research finds that girls do not read fiction for role models, rather "[engaging] with theme and form over character" (13). Feminist scholars and educators have every right to be concerned with problematic representations of female adolescent agency, but we should not discount girls' sophistication as readers since, as Blackford argues, they are attuned to formal and thematic matters associated with genre. For the English classroom, this means that teachers are in a unique position to encourage students, especially girls, to enhance their critical capacity through thinking, writing, and speaking about such complexities, skills that translate to scholarly, creative, and virtual realms, which the following section demonstrates.

Girls Respond: The Bella Cullen Project

As artists and producers of culture themselves, girls' creative work exemplifies their interpretive strategies, which do not enact passive role modeling, and reveals how girls are active creators of culture. Contradictions in mass-produced popular culture, especially paradoxical and controversial representations of girlhood, create a space for girls to re-negotiate the meaning in these adult-generated texts, a finding that has significant implications for the English classroom. Liza (thetwilightreader) not only creates short films that feature her speaking into the camera; she also animates *Twilight*-themed cartoons using software on her computer, makes puppets and coordinates skits, and acts in original parodies (for example, in "Jane Gym ... FEEL THE BURN!" Liza spoofs the villainous vampire Jane Volturi by pretending she is a rigorous personal trainer who demands exercise from her victims). Frequently noting her appreciation of the films' soundtracks, Liza also digitally edits music videos and even composes original lyrics to pre-existing melodies; this musical emphasis is shared by other girl fans of *Twilight*.

Including Chandler Nash (vocals, guitar, piano), Tori Randall (vocals, guitar), and Ally Kiger (vocals, bass guitar, percussion), The Bella Cullen Project is a musical trio that plays "Acoustic/TwiRock." According to the biography on their Facebook page, the band formed in 2007 when the three thirteen-and-fourteen-year-old best friends composed a *Twilight*-inspired song, "Sexy Vampire," during a sleepover. Based in Arlington, Texas, the group's public and global visibility among *Twilight* fans was not initially elevated through the endorsement of an adult with industry influence, but rather though the social network MySpace. After their first gig at a small-town bookstore's midnight release of *Eclipse* in 2007, the girls report:

> We soon had well over 1 million myspace profile views and song plays and even caught the attention of MTV and had our very own concert filmed by MTV and featured on TRL, including a music video of our song "Out of the Blue". Other media sources soon followed, such as ABC's Nightline, and we were also featured in popular magazines like CosmoGirl, Esquire and People Magazine. We traveled all over the country, performing for thousands of people along the way, and were privileged enough to meet many prominent people associated with the *Twilight* universe such as Stephenie Meyer, actor Robert Pattinson, and most of the other cast members from the *Twilight* Saga movies to name a few. (The Bella, *Facebook*)

Like Liza, the band's originally private artistic productions gained public visibility through online space. Their subsequent interaction with media giants provides a fitting example of how teen girls shape culture through their back-and-forth interaction with mass media. The Bella Cullen Project also provides an important exemplar of how girls engage texts.

First, as readers interpreting Meyer's text, The Bella Cullen Project imagines feelings and tensions associated with particular moments in the *Twilight* Saga through original lyrics and music characterized by vocal harmonies and acoustic guitars. This sympathetic perspective is not one that seeks to replicate or idolize Bella's actions, but to understand them in the context of the series. For example, in "It's Recreation, Not Suicide" the lyrics work out the contradictory implications associated with Bella's choice to cliff-dive in *New Moon*; while she later claims the activity is a recreational one, the reader knows Bella engages in the near-death action in order to hear Edward's voice in his absence. The song's chorus plays with these inconsistencies: "Tick tick tick / It's recreation, not suicide / When you told me you loved me, / Why did you lie? / Oh Sweet Edward, you're on my mind. / It's recreation, not suicide." Perhaps a clever twist on the word "recreation," the song may suggest Bella is tempting death in order to live. In another tune, the girl singer-songwriters adopt the alternate, dueling male perspectives of Edward and Jacob in "Vampwolf." The song's last verse overlaps Edward's chorus, "You smell like werewolf," with Jacob's chorus, "You smell like vampire." Merging the two perspectives demonstrates Edward's and Jacob's similar yearnings and replicates their tortured presence in Bella's own conflicted heart.

In addition to engaging with the *Twilight* Saga through affective interpretations that highlight situations of emotional complexity, The Bella Cullen Project's songs illustrate multiple characters' perspectives, as "Vampwolf" exemplifies. Their musical personas do not identify singularly with Bella's perspective (despite the name of the band). The song "Let it Go" adopts Jacob's point of view and is critical of Bella's indecisiveness:

> She's the kind of girl who wants her cake and wants to eat it, too / She's the kind of girl who wants you only when she's in the mood / She'll pull out all the stops to make you feel like you're on top / But you're lower than low / She's gonna lead you on and break your heart / And you won't even know.

Another song, "Victoria's Lament," adopts the perspective of the evil vampire Victoria, who returns in *Eclipse* to try to kill Bella as retribution for her lover James' death in *Twilight*. Sung in deeper, darker tones than other songs, the chorus threatens: "He's gone, she's not / Mate for mate she will be taught / How to finish someone off!" Nash, Randall, and Kiger's ability to dip into different characters' emotional lives and sing through these perspectives reflects a sophistication that disrupts role-model critiques. This example offers insight into girls' interpretive strategies, which often lean toward a preference for performance and conflict negotiation, rather than character identification, a finding that may inform approaches to engaging girls in the English classroom.

The Bella Cullen Project is another example of how pop culture, like *Twilight*, becomes an avenue to female friendships and future non-*Twilight* artistic endeavors. Neither "thetwilightreader" nor The Bella Cullen Project are currently pursuing their *Twilight*-themed art, but they are pursuing creative and scholarly projects. In the latter half of 2010, the focus of Liza's videos switched, in accordance with her new interests in pop culture, to music groups like the band Owl City. In 2011, Liza had a new channel under the name "LuckyLiza2" and she no longer posts videos related to *Twilight*. Similarly, Nash, Randall, and Kiger played their last concert as the "BCP" in 2009 at the *Twilight* fan convention in Dallas; as they have just recently graduated from high school, they are "bound for college next year" (Facebook). Now with her own professional musician's website, Nash will be attending the prestigious Liverpool Institute for Performing Arts, co-founded by legendary musician and former-Beatle Paul McCartney. These girls' examples prove that, instead of fearing girls' consumption of ideologically informed texts that may carry contradictory and controversial messages, educators and scholars, especially those invested in feminist activism, should celebrate the complexity that creates a space for real girls to act as agents of popular culture.

Conclusion

The *Twilight* Saga offers a window onto contemporary representations of adolescent girlhood in popular culture, especially given the series' connections to earlier literary works and contemporary texts. Exploring often-contradictory representations of female agency in popular culture requires a consideration of actual girls' engagements with mass media, particularly their agential negotiation of meaning with contemporary works as evidenced by Liza (thetwilightreader) and musical trio The Bella Cullen Project. While these are two extraordinary examples given their public personas, the interpretive strategies are consistent with the kinds of responses illustrated by girls on multiple fansites and forums dedicated to the *Twilight* Saga and other popular culture phenomena. Acting as both consumers and producers, girl fans' active relationships with texts like *Twilight* reveal how girls themselves transcend the dominant culture's perception of agency in girlhood.

Certainly, paradoxical and limiting messages about female agency are problematic, especially those simultaneously encouraging and constraining adolescent sexuality. Yet, as actual *Twilight* fans exemplify, feminist scholars and educators should be more confident in girls' ability to engage critically with—and to be artistically inspired by—those messages. Endorsing and incorporating an appreciation for popular culture, both mass media and the works female youth produce in response to them, will enrich the English classroom that seeks to empower and engage girls through relatable forums that they can embrace.

Acknowledgments

Portions of this chapter were presented in papers at two academic meetings: "'Team Edward!': Female Sexuality in Vampire Texts of 2008," Children's Literature Association Annual Conference (2009), and "'Can you just bite me?': Female Agency and Sexuality in *Twilight* Texts of 2008," Center for Women's and Gender Studies Graduate Student Conference at the University of Texas-Austin (2010). Special thanks to Dr. Marilynn Olson (Texas State University-San Marcos), Dr. Mary Celeste Kearney, and Dr. Dana Cloud (both University of Texas-Austin) for their insight into revisions of those papers.

Works Cited

Alcott, Louisa May. *Little Women*. New York: Signet Classic, 2004. Print.
The Bella Cullen Project. *Facebook*. Facebook. 2011. Web. 9 July 2011.
——"It's Recreation, Not Suicide." *Tick Tick Tick*. 2009. MP3.

——"Let It Go." *Tick Tick Tick.* 2009. MP3.

——"Vampwolf." *The Bella Cullen Project.* 2008. CD.

——"Victoria's Lament." *The Bella Cullen Project.* 2008. CD.

Blackford, Holly Virginia. *Out of This World: Why Literature Matters to Girls.* New York: Teachers College Press, 2004. Print.

Bowles-Reyer, Amy. "Becoming a Woman in the 1970s: Female Adolescent Sexual Identity and Popular Literature." *Growing up Girls: Popular Culture and the Construction of Identity.* Eds. Sharon Mazzarella and Norma Odom Pecora. New York: Peter Lang, 2001. 21–47. Print.

Brontë, Charlotte. *Jane Eyre* [1847]. Ed. Margaret Smith. Oxford: Oxford University Press, 2000. Print.

Durham, Meenakshi Gigi. "The Girling of America: Critical Reflections on Gender and Popular Communication." *Popular Communication* 1.1 (2003): 23–31. Print.

"Faith, Hope, and Trick." *Buffy the Vampire Slayer: The Complete Third Season,* 1999. Warner Brothers, 2003. DVD.

Fralic, Shelley. "Potter's Hermione Granger Is a Pop Culture Anomaly." *Vancouver Sun,* 16 Nov. 2010. Web. 30 Nov. 2010.

Gilbert, Sandra M. "*Jane Eyre* and the Secrets of Furious Lovemaking." *Novel: A Forum on Fiction* 31.3 (1998): 351–72. Print.

Griffin, Christine. "Good Girls, Bad Girls: Anglocentrism and Diversity in the Constitution of Contemporary Girlhood." *All about the Girl: Culture, Power, and Identity.* Ed. Anita Harris. New York: Routledge, 2004. 29–43. Print.

Harris, Anita. "The 'Can-Do' Girl versus the 'At-Risk' Girl." *Future Girl: Young Women in the Twenty-First Century.* New York: Routledge, 2004. Print.

Inness, Sherrie A. "Introduction." *Delinquents and Debutantes: Twentieth-Century American Girls' Cultures.* Ed. Sherrie A. Inness. New York: New York University Press, 1998. 1–15. Print.

Johnson, Alandra. "In Buffy vs. Bella, Buffy Slays as Role Model." *The Bulletin.* Western Communications, Inc. 22 May 2009. Web. 30 Nov. 2010.

Kapurch, Katie. "'Unconditionally and Irrevocably': Theorizing the Melodramatic Impulse in YA Literature through the *Twilight* Saga and *Jane Eyre.*" *Children's Literature Association Quarterly* 37.2 (2012): 164–87. Print.

Kearney, Mary Celeste. "Coalescing: The Development of Girls' Studies." *NWSA Journal* 21.1 (2009): 1–28. Print.

——*Girls Make Media.* New York: Routledge, 2006. Print.

——"Productive Spaces: Girls' Bedrooms as Sites of Cultural Production." *Journal of Children and Media* 1.2 (2007): 126–41. Print.

LuckyLiza2. YouTube. 1 Sept. 2010. Web. 30 June 2011.

Mazzarella, Sharon R. "Introduction." *Girl Wide Web: Girls, the Internet, and the Negotiation of Identity.* New York: Peter Lang, 2005. 1–12. Print.

Meyer, Stephenie. *Breaking Dawn.* New York: Little, Brown, 2008. Print.

——*Eclipse.* New York: Little, Brown, 2007. Print.

——"Frequently Asked Questions: *Breaking Dawn.*" Official Website of Stephenie Meyer. Web. 1 June 2009.

——*New Moon.* New York: Little, Brown, 2006. Print.

——*Twilight.* New York: Little, Brown, 2005. Print.

Nash, Chandler. Chandler Nash. Band Zoogle. Web. 9 July 2011.

Odem, Mary E. *Delinquent Daughters: Protecting and Policing Adolescent Female Sexuality in the United States, 1885–1920.* Chapel Hill, NC: University of North Carolina Press, 1995. Print.

O'Quinn, Elaine J. "Vampires, Changelings, and Radical Mutant Teens: What the Demons, Freaks, and Other Abominations of Young Adult Literature Can Teach Us about Youth." *The ALAN Review* 31.3 (2004): 50–56. Print.

Platt, Carrie Anne. "Cullen Family Values: Gender and Sexual Politics in the Twilight Series." *Bitten by Twilight: Youth Culture, Media, and the Vampire Franchise.* Eds. Melissa A. Click, Jennifer Stevens Aubrey, and Elizabeth Behm-Morawitz. New York: Peter Lang, 2010. Print.

Saxton, Ruth O. "Introduction." *The Girl: Constructions of the Girl in Contemporary Fiction by Women.* New York: St. Martin's Press, 1998. xi–xxix. Print.

Smith, Frank. *The Book of Learning and Forgetting.* New York: Teachers College Press, 1998. Print.

thetwilightreader. "10 Reasons Why I Love Twilight." YouTube. 10 Aug. 2009. Web. 1 Mar. 2010.

——"Jane Gym … FEEL THE BURN!" YouTube. 26 July 2009. Web. 1 Mar. 2010.

——"TheTwilightReader's Channel." YouTube. 7 Mar. 2009. Web. 1 Mar. 2010.

Twilight. Dir. Catherine Hardwicke. Perf. Kristen Stewart and Robert Pattinson. 2008. Summit Entertainment, 2009. DVD.

8

THE CHALLENGES OF TEACHING GIRLS (RE)PRESENTATION OF SELF AND OTHERS THROUGH MEDIA STUDIES AND CITIZEN JOURNALISM

Shayla Thiel-Stern

Girls and Media

At the top of media studies teacher Alyssa Maher's syllabus is this quotation:

> Freedom of the press is limited to those who own one (A.J. Liebling)

Most likely, Alyssa's students have never heard of Liebling or his work as a *New Yorker* reporter between the 1930s and 1960s, but the quote sets a mood for her unit on citizen journalism that any feminist scholar would appreciate. It echoes the disparities of power that keep the voiceless silent and tells of the need for enterprising citizens to overcome such limits. In an era when technological tools continue to be used to tip the scales of power, Liebling's message is a rallying call to teach the marginalized among us to seize these tools to express the freedom in question. Wisely, Alyssa recognizes that her high school class, made up mostly of girls of lower social-economic status and of varying races and ethnicities, is a proper place to begin unpacking Liebling's critical message.

By connecting the ways in which girls are represented by media with the ways they make sense of and produce media, I seek to present a framework that empowers them to use the tools of media practitioners for self-representation. Research conducted in two high school media studies classrooms opens up questions of how critical examination of race, gender, class, ethnicity, and other factors combined with the tools of interactive media informs attitudes about mass media and empowers students to create their own media messages. Let us first, however, consider some common perceptions about girls and media as we imagine how teachers might alert girls to ways media can work for or against them.

Mass Media Represents Girls

Mass media permeates the world of most adolescent girls, increasingly taking over a public space that offers constant audio visual stimulation and a private space where even staring alone at a cell phone offers personalized advertising messages. Adolescent girls are a focused target for content aimed to appeal to them even as it represents them in stereotypical, sexist ways. Mass media's representation of adolescent girls tends to overlook qualities like intelligence and creativity. Instead, it functions as a space where femininity is defined by sexiness (Durham 37), beauty (Currie 15), domesticity, and product consumption (McRobbie 263). Early on, girls are taught that a major goal of their adolescent years should be an idealized heterosexual romance (Christian-Smith 6) and the construction of a personal narrative consistent with such a romance (Davies 17), even though these hetereo-normative themes are frequently at odds with their true feelings (Finders 120). From celebrity icons to manufactured images in teen magazines, girls learn that appearance is a major key to "getting the guy" (Currie 64) and, generally, appearance is linked directly to retail products that will help achieve this.

From television, audiences get fictional girl characters that are ultra-feminine, popular, coiffed, and perfect in general (*Hannah Montana, Gossip Girl*) as well as young female reality "stars" framed in the same idealistic way (*The Hills, America's Next Top Model*). One of the most dominant mass media narratives of the feminine is that of the fairy-tale princess—Cinderella, Sleeping Beauty, and even Princess Fiona from *Shrek*—a narrative long valued by girls worldwide, as demonstrated by their fondness for wearing flowing costume dresses with tiaras (Orenstein 15). In the media, as in the classroom, the "good girl," who is nice, polite, and modest, is a cultural ideal that is difficult to attain and potentially harmful in its tendency to rob girls of assertive communication and leadership skills (Brown and Gilligan 78–80; Simmons 25). Adolescent girls from differing backgrounds, lifestyles, and cultures have an even more difficult time seeing themselves in mass media representations. Not only are they unable to fulfill the pre-defined and Photoshopped perfection of the gender roles presented to them, but also many have little to no representation within the media's image of the "perfect" teen because of race, ethnicity, sexuality, or religious differences.

Mass media representations of an American girl living the stereotypical American girlhood are not a new phenomenon, nor are media products that place girls directly in the role of culturally prescribed consumers. Teen girls living in the USA in the 1920s, 1930s, 1940s, and 1950s were typically identified in the media by their bobby sox and poodle skirts (Schrum 23), perceived hypersexuality (Nash 140–41), and "gabbiness" (Kearney "Birds" 570). Similar stereotypes endure through media representations of girls today. Although popular media products geared toward adolescent girls paint a specific depiction of them for purposes of consumption, news media represents girls somewhat differently. News stories often present girls as in crisis (Mazzarella and Pecora 7), depicting them as everything from helpless to mean. Carla Stokes (45) points out that Black American adolescent girls, especially, are presented with limited mass media options for themselves and are often represented as "hypersexual and deviant." Thiel-Stern has demonstrated how even news items about girls' use of the Internet can be categorized as stories about (A) girls who are attacked as victims online or (B) girls who flaunt too much sexuality, with the most troubling news stories (C) combining both images in a way that suggests that overtly sexual girls ask to be attacked by online predators ("Femininity out of Control" 35).

Girls' Digital (Re)Presentations

Despite news media's tendency to overreact to teen girls' online behaviors, recent developments in digital and interactive media present misrepresented adolescent girls with an opportunity to (re)present themselves in ways that are different from their popular images. As cultural producers of this new media (Mazzarella "Claiming" 142; Kearney *Girls Make Media* 15), girls are in a more powerful position than ever to resist mass culture's constructions of commercialized femininity and sexuality. The Internet has become a key place for girls to articulate sexuality, negotiate identity, navigate social relations, enact creativity, and simply communicate with the world around them—from the interactivity of creative postings on blogs, forums, and social networking sites to Instant Messaging conversations (Clark 218; Stern 230; Grisso and Weiss 36; Thiel-Stern 85).

Katherine Sweeney writes that "(t)he digital revolution has proven to be a great gender equalizer" (233) as compact digital video cameras and laptop editing software abound and, increasingly, as school and extracurricular programs are developed specifically to teach girls how to produce their own films (Sweeney 233–34; *Girls Make Media* 205). By simply logging on to Facebook or Google Sites, adolescent girls with access to the Internet can share lyrics, links, stories, and photos by clicking buttons; moreover, even girls limited in technological access because of income can obtain tools and view sites via mobile devices (Smith online). However, even though adolescent girls have unprecedented opportunities to (re)present themselves through new media, they often still do so using the discourse and presentation of the sexist patriarchal past. Some girls will chide one another online for being "sluts" or "lesbians" if they exercise excessive sexual agency in their remarks (Grisso and Weiss 39–40), and others simply fall into the gendered roles of mother/caretaker or vixen in their language with members of the opposite sex (Thiel-Stern *Instant Identity* 75), evidence that technological tools alone do not break ingrained cultural identities.

Feminist Pedagogy, Activity Theory, and *Bricolage*

In an analysis dependent upon understanding how race, gender, class, and other aspects of identity can be negotiated through the study and production of media, feminist pedagogy can function as a theoretical framework. Feminist pedagogy calls for the development of classroom strategies meant to empower those who are marginalized or powerless in the educational system (Fisher 35); this focus makes it an appropriate framework for the study of mixed-gender, multi-racial classrooms like the two analyzed later in this essay. Although neither of the teachers whose classrooms are described identified feminist pedagogy as a specific part of an overall teaching philosophy, it is clear that the teaching styles and goals of both fall within the boundaries of feminist pedagogy.

Roger Simon refers to such pedagogical styles as "pedagog[ies] of possibility," noting they also include the ability to "interrogate both social forms and their possible transformations" with regard to the principles of diversity and compassionate justice (23). Simon's principles offer a perfect counter-argument that provides a means to further understanding how the news media covers groups and communities in its stories, a critical discernment in a media studies classroom. Furthermore, a pedagogy that teaches students to think critically about not only media but also their own actions allows for the potential transformation Simon points toward. As bell hooks writes: "Without the capacity to think critically about ourselves and our lives, none of us would be able to move forward, to change, to grow" (202). Keeping in mind the tenets of feminist pedagogy and how they emerge in classroom dynamics, the two classrooms discussed illuminate how such strategies can be employed in studies of media to allow the articulation of self-chosen identities, equitably uncover the identities of others, and use what is learned to speak back to mass media. My study of these two classrooms also reveals the social and academic shortcomings of and future possibilities for new media, specifically as it relates to girls, and illustrates how aspects of race, ethnicity, gender, sexuality, and class, which are connected directly to issues of cultural power and identity, manifest themselves in the classroom.

Answering complicated questions about issues of power and identity calls for what Lévi-Strauss (1974) terms *bricolage*, or personally piecing together different cultural artifacts to understand a story more completely (16). As a participant-observer, I worked closely with two passionate teachers and their students over two different periods of time. It is tempting to set up binaries in any comparative analysis, but I borrow instead from activity theory, which relies upon humans' ability to be active agents and presents a framework where activities, and thus analysis, are viewed as goal-directed or purposeful (Engestrom 26; Davydov 39). Activity theory is useful because it allows us to consider that, in addition to a set of pre-existing conditions and rules (such as different classroom technologies, administrative hierarchies, teaching strategies), the teachers in this study had different goals and their students likewise had different goals for themselves (Roth and Tobin 114). Wolff-Michael Roth and Kenneth Tobin write that a key tenet of activity theory is

> the transformations of individuals and their community, which result from
> the fact that human beings do not merely react to their life conditions but

that they have the power to act and therefore the power to change the very conditions that mediate their activities,

an idea grounded firmly in Marxism (1–2). Given the feminist pedagogical goal of transformation, these two theories work well together; however, feminists also acknowledge the crucial and real discrepancies of social, cultural, and political power inherent in the educational system, and, often, in the context of institutions, power is relative. Not everyone has the power to change all the conditions that mediate their activities in this perspective. Keeping in mind these varying view-points, my study utilizes a *bricolage* of my own observations, interviews with students and teachers, and the work produced by the students to better understand the complex interplay of identity issues and new media in the classroom.

Two Classroom Perspectives

Media Studies and Online Journalism, 2009

In 2009, I met Erin Hansen, a veteran English teacher, who had recently spear-headed a new digital media focused curriculum for Kennedy High School, a diverse public school in the Twin Cities. Although learning to do journalism was not a major component of the curriculum of her courses in documentary film and media studies, Erin saw it as a means for students to represent themselves—to bring visibility to their school and community. The school could not financially support a print student newspaper or a class devoted to newspaper production, so I volunteered to teach students journalism and the digital media skills necessary to produce an online newspaper. Additionally, Erin taught them to produce video news programs that could be shown regularly in homeroom and distributed to the Twin Cities community on cable access television and the Internet.

Erin presented the idea of a student-produced monthly online newspaper to her media studies class. She then announced that I would be teaching basic journalism and Web production skills during the lunch period (offering free pizza as an added incentive). Several students seemed exceptionally excited, and about fifteen students attended the workshop, including a few student government representatives who saw a school newspaper as an opportunity to promote their own work. In teaching interviewing techniques and inverted pyramid style writing, Erin and I reminded students that what they were learning as they worked in their digital media studies classes also applied to their work as journalists: They should strive to be objective; they should allow people (especially those who are often voiceless) to speak for themselves; and they should see this as an opportunity to get important stories and information to their community while also learning valuable production skills.

The first two workshop sessions on traditional newsgathering, interviewing, and news writing went well. Students were engaged and having fun. They worked together to generate ideas for the online newspaper and looked forward to embedding their digital videos in stories and promoting their work to peers through social media sites. The group was exciting to work with because of its diversity, which included boys and girls (though mostly girls) who were African-American, Somali-American Muslim, Caucasian, Latina, and Asian-American. Girls took the lead on most aspects of the work to be done, though each student had a potentially interesting story to tell. We encouraged students to include first-person blogs and to supplement news and feature stories with audio podcasts or video, seeing this as an opportunity to hone technical skills and also articulate gender and racial identities.

I asked students to use some of the lessons they learned in their classes with Erin—specifically, the understanding that journalists should strive to be as fair as possible, especially important since people are sometimes unfairly represented in the media or not represented at all. Erin also engaged students in discussions about mass media and representation. Once, she reminded them of a discussion they had had in their media studies and documentary film classes about what it meant to "frame" a story or tell it in a way that suited the storyteller's aims. One student, an African-American junior girl named Renee, admitted to Erin she saw no connection between this film class lesson and journalism:

> "Ms. Hansen? We watched *Grizzly Man* [a documentary about a man who lived in the Alaskan wilderness with bears] and that was about that guy Treadwell who was really pretty crazy, and he was eaten up by a bear. I don't see what that has to do with this."
>
> "Renee, think about what the director, Herzog, was trying to tell the audience about Timothy Treadwell and obsession, and remember how he just showed his family watching the footage of him being killed? Think about the powerful ways that you can tell important stories as you work using what you're learning about journalism."

Renee merely shrugged. She said she had chosen *Grizzly Man* as the documentary that her group analyzed for class, but admitted she had a difficult time relating to the story and to the man who was the subject. We encouraged her to think about subjects that she did relate to in her journalism work. However, since the after-school (there was work that needed to be done beyond the lunch hour) journalism project was not actually connected to Renee's classes, this tie challenged her.

Although critical connections to the curriculum and media studies topics were important from a learning standpoint, Erin also wanted students to feel connected to the work produced for the digital newspaper. "I really want this to increase the sense of community and school spirit at Kennedy," she said. "This is *your* school newspaper." Erin then developed a contract for students to solidify their commitment to this extracurricular venture, outlining expectations such as "strong work ethic and commitment to learning about journalism, good attendance and passing grades in all classes, attendance to one after-school work session per week," and other attendance-related rules.

Twelve students, nine females and three males, returned signed contracts and seemed committed to the newspaper. However, technology itself often impeded progress. Although the school and district agreed to allow students in the digital media studies program to use YouTube and social networking in class, the sites were "blocked" through the first two startup weeks, so we were unable to upload video or promote any of the student work. Moreover, Erin decided that, rather than rely upon the free online template offered by the National High School Press Association, students would design their own Web pages using Dreamweaver, a popular program used to build and publish Web sites. After a slow software installation process and countless technical issues, student attention waned. Although we continued the once-a-week workshop that I taught and the two after-school sessions that Erin oversaw, only a core group of five juniors remained on our digital newspaper staff after the first month: two Caucasian girls, one African-American girl, one Latina girl, and one Caucasian boy, who only made it to one after-school session before he left for other extracurricular activities. Many of the original students, and specifically the Somali girls, could not commit to an after-school activity because they had to catch a bus to another part of the city immediately after school where they had responsibilities at home.

Our core group of five students worked on stories about lunchroom controversies, homecoming festivities, sports, and feature pieces on new teachers and students. They shot their own digital photos and video and built personal Web pages. Erin believed that the best way for students to make the most impact on the student body and larger community was to produce a professional quality online newspaper with stories that used a traditional news writing style. After another month of work, the girls had produced enough stories, blog entries, and video clips to create a full first issue, and, in individual interviews conducted with them, seemed proud of their work. However, despite our emphasis on identity construction, none of the blogs focused on gender, race, or class, or took advantage of the opportunity to (re)present these aspects of identity differently than the mainstream media might have. An example comes from Renee:

> I wrote a story about homecoming, but then I also wrote a blog about how students really don't get into homecoming (at Kennedy) like they did at a school that I used to go to, and just that it's too bad. Look, I posted some pictures from homecoming from my last school last year, and you can just see that people are a lot more into it.

Another student, Taylor, remarked she was "writing a story about a kid from our school who was from Somalia and who people think went back over there to fight in the war or something." Although this was an important and truly incredible story that was widely reported in the Twin Cities (and, eventually, by national media),

Taylor had not received quotes from any reliable sources, and much of her piece was just hearsay. We encouraged her to reference what we had discussed in class about being critical of sources and seeking "official" sources, but to the best of my knowledge she never went back and did this.

One of the other girls, Jacqueline, realized she had a talent for design and layout and offered to create a home page for all of the other students' stories. Erin loaned her the classroom laptop for the project. We decided to reconvene after the work was finished, and I encouraged Jacqueline to email me if she became stuck on any technical issues. A number of weeks later, I received an email from Erin, who had become increasingly frustrated with the digital newspaper project. She said that Taylor, who "was most committed to leading the production," had become pregnant and dropped out of Kennedy to attend an alternative school. Jacqueline, on the other hand, had kept Erin's laptop and not shown up for school for three weeks. I later learned that when she returned, the computer screen was cracked. Shortly afterward, she too transferred to an alternative school.

Erin finally sent me this communication:

> I am really unable to carry this load at this point. My other duties are too much. I promised myself that if the kids didn't do the work, I would not end up doing it for them. I have to let it go for the year, I think. I hate doing that, but I think for the sake of my health, I need to.

I agreed, and we decided to meet over the summer to discuss whether the digital newspaper project could be re-launched the following year, perhaps using classtime or through a grant. However, Erin resigned her position, so we did not connect again. Kennedy received funding the following year for an English teacher to oversee a journalism class, but after a year he was laid off because of budget cuts. In retrospect, I do not think this overall experience was at all atypical, but will consider conclusions later in light of the second classroom media experience.

Media Studies and Hyperlocal Citizen Journalism, 2011

In December 2011, I connected with Alyssa Maher, the new digital media studies teacher at Kennedy. After a short two years, the program looked quite different. Many of the original teachers and administrators had departed; however, many of the curricular goals remained the same. Like Erin, Alyssa was committed to teaching her students critical media literacy skills along with how to produce their own media in the media studies and documentary film classes. Both teachers shared many of the same materials, including some of the same documentaries and topical units, though their classroom styles were different. Perhaps the biggest change was that classroom technology had evolved and improved over the past two years. All students had access to computers, iPod Touches, and video cameras, and more free sites had been developed where students could upload their own work. Although

the diversity of the students involved in the program remained, Alyssa's media studies class had nearly an equal number of girls and boys, though that did not change
the fact that the girls still seemed more engaged.

After the journalism teacher was laid off, no plans were made to continue to
publish a student newspaper. However, Alyssa saw this as an opportunity to revisit a
critical study of journalism production in her class. She wanted students to understand citizen journalism, a method of journalism production that had been cata-
pulted into the spotlight in 2010 and 2011 as citizens posted their own media on
social networking sites like Twitter, and launched revolutions in Egypt, Tunisia,
and other parts of the Arab world. Since many of Alyssa's students identified as
Muslim and had family members living in Africa, she felt they would find this
especially relevant. She saw citizen journalism, hyperlocal journalism (the idea of
providing intense heavy news coverage in a very small space or community), and
blogging as a way for students to look beyond local television news as a main source
of media information. We both saw these new media tools as a potentially
empowering site for all.

Alyssa suggested we co-facilitate the unit on digital journalism much in the same
way that I had with Erin, but this time as a five-week in-class unit instead of as a
lunchtime/after-school project. Students could choose teams that would produce
hyperlocal online news publications, and they would compete with one another for
an opportunity to be taken to lunch by Alyssa and me. They would receive points
for stories, photos, blog entries, Twitter, videos, and podcasts included on their sites,
as well as for writing and production quality. Only one class period would be spent
learning to use Google Sites (a free template for creating and uploading sites)
because students were already familiar with Google layout and tools from regular
classroom use of Google Documents. Each group chose a name for their publication, and, as in the 2009 project, girls began to emerge as leaders of each of the four
groups, making lists of story ideas, distributing them, and volunteering to design
front pages and act as editors.

In our first session, I passed out sections of local and national newspapers to students and asked for notes on what they saw there in terms of layout, writing style,
and story topics. I showed several video clips of television news stories and examples
of multimedia news stories, again asking about the differences in storytelling, visual
presentation, and what the stories communicated to audiences. Students then went
to the computers to seek out examples of hyperlocal reporting and citizen journalism (they had several sites to choose from) and discuss the differences they observed.
Although we spent class time discussing journalistic writing conventions and newsgathering, students mostly concentrated on planning publications and assigning
stories, photos, and videos to individual team members.

Like Erin, Alyssa encouraged students to consider ways to represent themselves as
citizen journalists that were not possible through traditional media. She asked them
to think about writing stories pertaining to their school and home communities that
they might not see on the local TV news. She reminded them of a previous unit on

"food deserts" (areas in the industrialized world where healthy, affordable food is difficult to obtain), and how poor urban areas were generally affected, and asked them to consider similar topics that would be appealing to their communities but were not covered extensively elsewhere. After this nudging, two of the Latina (female) students began a short story and strong blog entry on the DREAM (Development, Relief and Education for Alien Minors) Act, a piece of legislation that was currently before the U.S. Senate and meant to provide conditional U.S. residency for high school students in good legal standing who wanted to attend college or the military, but whose parents were illegal immigrants. Additional stories included topical issues such as teen pregnancy within Kennedy High School, gun control among minors and gang members, and the recent firing of a popular administrator. Media about extracurricular events was also produced. Many of the students tended to work quietly in their groups, staring intently at computer screens for most of the class period, and occasionally asking one another if they had finished their part of the team's work for the day. At the end of most class periods, the majority of students kept working at their computers even though class had ended.

Alyssa noted in an interview with me that she saw students beginning to make connections to earlier lessons in their media studies class:

> As students developed their Web sites, they attempted to avoid publishing propaganda or advertising for events, products, or ideas. Furthermore, thanks to a unit on representation in the media, students were also aware of the power of writing and publication. In their writing, they aimed to resist stereotypes and produce media that was somewhat alternative and, simultaneously, highly creative.

However, it was their enthusiasm for the assignment that most heartened Alyssa. "I've never seen them like this!" she said. "I wish they would do a better job of proofreading their work, but they are really into the reporting aspect of this."

One of the students, an African-American girl named Jasmine, was commended for her quick work in writing a breaking news story about a rash of tornadoes that ripped through a low-income Twin Cities neighborhood. As we scrolled through her story, another team member, a quiet Asian-American girl named Ava, pointed to one of the pictures and said, "That house? Right there? With all the trees that fell down in front of it? That's my house. We were in it." She said she was still shaken and even though her house was "fine," her entire family was staying indefinitely with her grandmother. Ava later wrote a blog post to accompany the news story in which she recounted grabbing a sleeping baby brother from his crib and running to the basement as the house trembled. Her story's repeated theme of her dad calling from work and asking only "Where's my son?" (rather than "How are you and your mom?") added a troubling aspect to the narrative, but seemed to be an important thread in Ava's story.

Alyssa elaborated on the final outcomes of the pieces as she saw them, specifically as they related to gender, race, and class and the appropriateness of these identifiers being included in a journalistic project.

> In my opinion, I think these social categories influenced both the manner in which the students worked in peer groups as well as the citizen journalism they produced. In nearly all the groups, a female student willingly accepted the leadership role and ultimately took responsibility for meeting the assignment deadlines. That said, the Web sites' content varied as student journalists of different backgrounds chose the topics to cover. For example, a couple of groups published stories on a recent student led protest for immigration rights. As actual participants in this particular protest, the students' writing was highly biased. Yet, under the guise of citizen journalism (as opposed to "traditional" journalism), the project was intended to be an outlet for the students to articulate their passion about topics that mattered to them personally. In this way, of course, social categories and factors heavily influenced their work.

In using a pedagogy that was both critical in its understanding of media and also feminist in that it allowed the female group leaders to fulfill learning objectives based on intersections of gender and racial identification, Alyssa's learning outcomes for her class were fulfilled, and her students seemed excited about the productive nature of their learning. This quotation from junior Sofia, a Latina student and group leader/editor, demonstrates a critical connection:

> I think that online media like what we did in class is important because sometimes people don't know the whole entire truth about the news and what's going on, so their news will not be fully accurate or they will be missing the big details. Most of the time they don't read between the lines and really get in depth with it like you can with this.

In many ways, Sofia provides a strong example of how untold "truths" and dominant media representations of gender (as well as race and class) can be (re)presented in the students' own words by using the tools of citizen journalism. Although female students in both classes never referenced gender specifically, it was implicit in many of their stories and blog entries, and femininity manifested itself in varied ways.

Classroom Implications for Girls and Media

Although the class projects in the two case studies were not intended to use feminist teaching practices or specifically illuminate how gender, race, and other social and cultural identifiers could be used within media studies, both did so to varying degrees. Given this chapter's earlier discussion about the unfair, sexist media portrayals of adolescent girls, teaching girls about feminist practices that look at media critically and then arming them with the tools necessary to produce their own digital media are important goals. As was clear in both groups, girls readily took on leadership roles with critical sensibilities about identity and community. While activity theory would posit that learning and transformation are dependent upon myriad cultural and institutional factors, these cases provide examples of how feminist pedagogy, and new media production specifically, can be used to empower girls. In the first case study, the teacher viewed the work as "failed" because of the lack of a final, professional project (and an unfair burden on herself to "reach" the female students). In the second study, the teacher viewed the work as "successful" because it fulfilled some of the broader goals of identity and community related to media studies as a whole.

In the 2009 study, a gender issue—Taylor becoming pregnant and dropping out—was one of the main reasons Erin felt the class journalism project failed. Additionally, another sense of failure arose when some of the Somali female students showed interest in the work but were unable to participate in afterschool activities because of their responsibilities at home. Arguably, Erin used a feminist pedagogical grounding and, ultimately, sacrificed her own time (and, in her words, "health") in order to be as accommodating as possible to students she knew faced challenges related to gender, race, and socio-economic status. She voluntarily added three days of after-school advising for the newspaper and asked students to commit to only one of those days, feeling it would be unrealistic to ask for more. She also loaned her laptop to a girl who did not have home access to a computer to complete the work.

Although Erin said she did not see her actions as sacrifices, she decided it was impossible to continue to lead the newspaper project because students seemed unmoved by her extra efforts, perhaps because they were too overwhelmed by their personal situations to see the generosity and energy offered by Erin. Little in the literature of feminist pedagogy relates to teacher burn-out or personal sacrifice as harmful, a shortcoming to be considered in this instance and others, as women traditionally bear the brunt of care and mothering in institutions of various types. On a more positive note, it is important to acknowledge that students in Erin's class were able to learn valuable technology and software skills they would not have otherwise learned. They also learned how mainstream media gathers news and constructs stories. This knowledge is valuable in terms of critical media literacy, but should also serve students well in future schooling or careers where they are responsible for constructing professional messages and images for audiences.

In retrospect, I question my own privileging of traditional news reporting and storytelling devices (rather than teaching students to effectively use blogs, social media, or methods of citizen journalism), and consider the choices I made in working with Erin's students as partly to blame for the project's failed outcomes. Had we inspired students to take stories from their own lives and tell them in ways meaningful to them, we might have truly performed feminist pedagogy, or provided a better means for students marginalized by gender, race, ethnicity, and class to feel empowered by new storytelling forms in new media. Furthermore, Erin's decision to use the more advanced Web design tools did grant students greater technical expertise and control, but also left them mired in technical issues they could not solve, causing many of them to grow frustrated with the process. This too could have been prevented, had I better anticipated the problem and spoken to Erin about it.

By making the citizen journalism unit a graded part of her media studies curriculum, and by relying upon a personalized, more casual, more familiar storytelling form produced through a Google product with which the students were already familiar, Alyssa in 2011 seemed immediately to overcome some of the issues faced by Erin and her class. She, too, was sensitive to students' needs to negotiate their identity in the classroom and online. However, instead of intensely focusing on individual students' circumstances as they related to gender and race, Alyssa allowed the issues to be intrinsically evoked through classroom dynamics and leadership skills and through the stories they produced for their hyperlocal citizen journalism sites. Like Erin, she expressed disappointment in the lack of professional presentation and quality in the sites, but we were both impressed by the way students produced visual, written, broadcast, and audio media about issues that were important to them and their communities. The girls in Alyssa's class in particular seemed to shine in the assignment. The "winning" team was made up entirely of girls and was the group that included stories about a woman administrative leader within the high school, teen pregnancy, the DREAM Act, and a personal photo journal essay from one of the girls who had been on a school bus during the I-35 Bridge collapse in Minneapolis in 2007.

Both case studies leave practitioners with important considerations as they use new media studies in the classroom in a way that is mindful of gender, race, and class. I suggest that such media projects, especially those allowing students to produce media in a way that is personal to them, also include an expressed framework that helps articulate identity—especially important for those who do not always get to tell their stories, such as Ava, who wrote about being caught in the tornado. While activity theory can generate rules for transformation through classroom tools and critical thinking exercises, a feminist pedagogy allows teachers to empower individual students and encourage them to make connections from their lives to the larger world of media, community, and culture. This framework, combined with digital media production, can truly make it possible for the girls who might otherwise be marginalized and misrepresented to (re)present themselves to audiences. Also, it seems important to understand that student life situations, time constraints, and family commitments will not be overcome simply because they are handed the tools of technology. Where, how, and when these tools are given clearly matter in any classroom. Teachers cannot necessarily change situations, but being mindful of them can open doors that make a difference.

Works Cited

Brown, Lyn Mickel, and Carol Gilligan. *Meeting at the Crossroads: Women's Psychology and Girls' Development*. Cambridge, MA: Harvard University Press, 1992. Print.

Christian-Smith, Linda K. *Texts of Desire: Essays on Fiction, Femininity and Schooling*. New York: Routledge Falmer, 1993. Print.

Clark, Lynn Scofield. "The Constant Contact Generation: Exploring Teen Friendships with Networks Online." *Girl Wide Web: Girls, the Internet, and the Negotiation of Identity*. Ed. Sharon Mazzarella. New York: Peter Lang, 2005. 203–20. Print.

Currie, Dawn. *Girl Talk: Adolescent Magazines and Their Readers*. Toronto: University of Toronto Press, 1999. Print.

Davies, Bronwyn. *Shards of Glass: Children Reading and Writing beyond Gendered Identities*. London: Hampton Press, 1993. Print.

Davydov, Vassily. "The Content and Unsolved Problems of Activity Theory." *Perspectives on Activity Theory*. Eds. Yrgo Engestrom, Reijo Miettinen, and Raija-Leena Punamaki. Cambridge, UK: Cambridge University Press, 1999. 39–50. Print.

Durham, Meenakshi Gigi. *The Lolita Effect: The Media Sexualization of Young Girls and What We Can Do about It*. New York: Overlook Press, 2008. Print.

——"The Taming of the Shrew: Women's Magazines and the Regulation of Desire." *Journal of Communication Inquiry* 20 (1996): 18–31. Print.

Engestrom, Yrgo. "Activity Theory and Social Transformation." *Perspectives on Activity Theory*. Eds. Yrgo Engestrom, Reijo Miettinen, and Raija-Leena Punamaki. Cambridge, UK: Cambridge University Press, 1999. 19–38. Print.

Finders, Margaret. *Just Girls: Hidden Literacies and Life in Junior High*. New York: Teachers College Press, 1997. Print.

Fisher, Bernice Malka. *No Angel in the Classroom: Teaching through Feminist Discourse*. New York: Rowman & Littlefield, 2001. Print.

Grisso, Ashley, and David Weiss. "What Are gURLs Talking about?" *Girl Wide Web: Girls, the Internet, and the Negotiation of Identity*. Ed. Sharon Mazzarella. New York: Peter Lang, 2005. 31–50. Print.

hooks, bell. *Teaching to Transgress: Education as the Practice of Freedom*. New York: Routledge, 1994. Print.

Kearney, Mary Celeste. "Birds on the Wire: Troping Teenage Girlhood through Telephony in Mid-Twentieth-Century U.S. Media Culture." *Cultural Studies* 19.5 (2005): 568–601. Print.

——*Girls Make Media*. New York: Routledge, 2007. Print.

——"New Directions: Girl-Centered Media Studies for the Twenty-First Century." *Journal of Children and Media* 2.1 (2008): 82–83. Print.

——"Recycling Judy and Corliss: Transmedia Exploitation and the First Teen-Girl Production Trend." *Feminist Media Studies* 4.3 (2004): 265–95. Print.

Lévi-Strauss, Claude. *The Savage Mind*. Trans. George Weidenfeld and Nicolson Ltd. Chicago, IL: University of Chicago Press, 1974. Print.

McRobbie, Angela. "Jackie: An Ideology of Adolescent Feminism." *Popular Culture: Past and Present*. Eds. Tony Bennett, Graham Martin, and Bernard Waites. London: Open University Press, 1982. 263–83. Print.

Mazzarella, Sharon R. "Claiming a Space: The Cultural Economy of Teen Girl Fandom on the Web." *Girl Wide Web: Girls, the Internet, and the Negotiation of Identity*. Ed. Sharon Mazzarella. New York: Peter Lang, 2005. 141–60. Print.

Mazzarella, Sharon R. and Norma Pecora. "Girls in Crisis: Newspaper Coverage of Adolescent Girls." *Journal of Communication Inquiry* 35.2 (2007): 6–27. Print.

Nash, Ilana. *American Sweethearts: Teenage Girls in Twentieth-Century Popular Culture*. Bloomington, IN: Indiana University Press, 2006. Print.

Orenstein, Peggy. *Cinderella Ate My Daughter: Dispatches from the Frontlines of the New Girlie-Girl Culture*. New York: Harper, 2011. Print.

Roth, Wolff-Michael, and Kenneth Tobin. "Redesigning an Urban Teacher Education Program: An Activity Theory Perspective." *Mind, Culture, and Activity* 9.2 (2002): 108–31. Print.

Schrum, Kelly. *Some Wore Bobby Sox: The Emergence of Teenage Girls' Culture, 1920–1945.* New York: Palgrave MacMillan, 2004. Print.

Simmons, Rachel. *The Curse of the Good Girl: Raising Authentic Girls with Courage and Confidence.* New York: Penguin, 2009. Print.

Simon, Roger. *Teaching against the Grain: Texts for a Pedagogy of Possibility.* New York: Bergen and Garvey, 1992. Print.

Smith, Aaron. "Mobile Access 2010." The Pew Internet and American Life Project. 7 July 2010. Web.

Stern, Susannah R. "Virtually Speaking: Girls' Self-Disclosure on the WWW." *Women's Studies in Communication* 25.2 (2002): 223–53.

Stokes, Carla E. "How Black American Adolescent Girls Construct Identity and Negotiate Sexuality on the Internet." *Girl Wide Web 2.0: Revisiting Girls, the Internet and the Negotiation of Identity.* Ed. Sharon R. Mazzarella. New York: Peter Lang, 2010. 45–68. Print.

Sweeney, Katherine. *Maiden U.S.A.: Girl Icons Come of Age.* New York: Peter Lang, 2008. Print.

Thiel-Stern, Shayla. "Femininity out of Control on the Internet: A Critical Analysis of Media Representations of Gender, Youth, and MySpace.com in International News Discourses." *Girlhood Studies* 2.1 (2009): 20–39. Print.

——*Instant Identity: Adolescent Girls and the World of Instant Messaging.* New York: Peter Lang, 2007. Print.

PART IV

Feminism and English Classroom Practices

9

COMPLICATING GENDER BINARIES IN THE FEMINIST ENGLISH CLASSROOM

Karen Coats and Roberta Seelinger Trites

For at least forty years, teachers have theorized about how to empower girls in the literature classroom—and the solution for many has been to engage feminist pedagogies. In this chapter, we trace how issues of critical thinking have led feminism (and misunderstandings of feminism) to intersect with secondary English education in the United States in order to contextualize a study we conducted of four high school teachers who self-consciously problematize gender while attempting to expose issues of critical thinking in their literature classrooms. We follow our consideration of texts and teachers with a demonstration of how two Young Adult (YA) novels marketed to girls—E. Lockhart's *The Disreputable History of Frankie Landau-Banks* and Suzanne Collins' *The Hunger Games*—represent gender as a multivariate social construct.

Our findings lead us to believe that YA novels provide a way for teachers to purposefully lead students to analyze feminism in terms of critical thinking—including asking students to think about issues of language, community, identity, and empowerment—because neither girls nor boys can effectively engage with social justice when they rely on stereotypes about gender and feminism. Most important, we find that a review of the literature on feminism and high school classrooms, a teacher survey we conducted, and the novels we investigate all demonstrate the importance of validating emotions in the teaching of social justice. Researchers and teachers indicate that adolescents (both female and male) who engage in empathetic understandings of situations and issues seem better prepared to understand how social problems, gender included, are created. Since YA novels tend to engage adolescent readers on many levels, including an emotional one, they provide ample opportunities for teaching critical thinking that is personal, analytical, and complex.

The Research

Ira Shor demonstrates that the 1983 *A Nation at Risk* (*Nation*) report generated multiple reforms in secondary education, including those that led to greater emphasis on critical thinking and critical reading for social justice issues, gender included (1). *Nation* identified students' inability to think critically as a fundamental weakness in the public educational system. Much of the research to follow was influenced by *Nation*'s reliance on concerns about stereotypes and various binaries, such as "male/female," "privileged/underprivileged," or even "right/wrong." For example, Gail Flynn's early feminist pedagogical work on gendered reading strategies among late adolescents shows male readers "rejecting" or "dominating" stories because they cannot empathize with them, whereas "women are often receptive to texts in that they attempt to understand them before making a judgment upon them" (251). While dividing readers into two types, male and female readers, Flynn also privileges concepts of critical thinking and critical reading skills as the "right" way to read: interpretation works best in her judgment when "self and other, reader and text, interact in such a way that the reader learns from the experience without losing critical distance" (237). This last sounds laudable as an articulated goal, but Flynn's language elsewhere betrays what she perceives as right and wrong ways of approaching texts; that is, critical thinking and reading belong to the receptive approach ascribed to her female readers, while perceived patterns of rejection, dominance, and lack of empathy are the habit of male readers. In this economy of binary equivalences, then, *Nation*'s desire for citizens "to reach some common understandings on complex issues" becomes an excuse to rely on stereotypes rather than foster new pedagogies.

In another argument based on the "right/wrong" binary that critical thinking pedagogies sometimes engage, Margaret Anne Zeller Carlson argues that books by and about women need to be included in the high school literature curriculum so that girls and boys can "learn to recognize each other in new ways" (30). Her concern is primarily focused on literature and its ability to liberate people from past stereotypes—but it also involves the dualistic thinking of male/female and right/wrong ways of reading.

Additionally, several scholars in Nancy Mellin McCracken and Bruce C. Appleby's 1992 *Gender Issues in the Teaching of English* demonstrate that some of the emphasis on using gender to teach critical thinking leads to unintentionally reinforced gender stereotypes. Nancy R. Comley reads a Hemingway text with students to demonstrate how, "as a binary opposition, birth and death are linked in this story to another binary, women and men" (79); Cynthia Ann Bowman generalizes: "girls' responses in their learning logs reflect nurturing, patient, sharing individuals, where the boys' logs show very practical, judgmental, and impatient people" (87); McCracken herself advocates teaching girls *and* boys "to read as girls"—just like girls have been taught to read like boys ("Re-gendering" 55).

One reason for this stark divide between female and male reading perspectives may be that the literature itself is infused with gender stereotypes; Hemingway, for instance, is not known for his enlightened views on gender issues, which is why we advocate for teaching YA texts such as the ones we examine later. Such texts complicate the social construction of gender in ways that raise questions rather than assume answers about identity and empowerment. However, it is important to note that if the reaction to *Nation* served to increase public awareness of the importance of social justice in general, then teaching a more gender-balanced literature curriculum in particular was a practical and expedient means to a broader end. Feminists wisely hitched their wagons to contemporary intellectual trends, unsuspecting that gender could then become only one more binary by which critical thinking skills were taught.

In 1992 the AAUWEF's report *How Schools Shortchange Girls* effected another series of reforms that this time were specific to educating girls. This report influenced many English teachers to reconsider how language and coded stereotype messages replicate gender stereotypes in English classes (St. Pierre 31). The result was a movement from binary thinking about gender to more complex and multivariate forms of interpretation. For example, in 1997 Megan Boler critiqued Freirean models that rationalize and politicize learning, noting that they may be inadequate in situations where students have an emotional response that prohibits new learning (417). Her argument, especially pertinent to feminist educational theory, asserts that teachers should "take account of ... the affective dimensions of our speech [and] the affective intensities and expressions of our bodies – gesture, rhythm, movement" (417). Boler argues that emotions, even unwieldy ones that are not easily identified by language, share a role in education.

The *English Journal* in 1999 also showcased work important to a feminist pedagogy of literature, including an examination of gendered discourse, collaboration, and restructured classroom spaces (O'Donnell-Allen and Smagorinsky); an interrogation of gender difference (Croker); gender as a social construct (McClure); and problematic language that replicates stereotypes (Cleary and Whittemore). No longer could gender be studied just as a means to an end such as (binaristic) critical thinking. Moreover, feminist thinkers were increasingly embracing the relationship between identity and critical thinking. By 2006, Janet Alsup could argue in *Teacher Identity Discourses* that although training teachers to think about their identities is "difficult, messy, and complex," the most successful teachers are those willing to problematize their identities within their classrooms (5). This meant that subject matter and how students thought about it were no longer the only culprits in influencing critical thinking skills.

Another important analysis of the relationship between teachers who are not self-conscious about their identity and binary thinking emerged in Mark Bracher's *Radical Pedagogy: Identity, Generativity, and Social Transformation*. He argues that in pedagogies focused on resistance and protest, "teachers seek recognition for their own identity vulnerability or deprivation, or that of a subaltern group with which they have identified, and oppose the authorities and establishment systems that are presumably responsible for this deficiency" (95). The goals of such pedagogies are to gain recognition for what he calls the "identity damage" of the group under study, to expose systems and master signifiers responsible for that damage, and to acquire new master signifiers that allow group members to recognize, enact, and re-value aspects of their identity that previously were oppressed, repressed, or alienated. In terms of gender, the goals expressed in the early feminist literature surveyed above serve these exact ends: to guide students toward understanding the systematic devaluing of women and female perspectives in literary texts, to locate the systems and signifiers responsible, and to enact new ways of thinking that enable students to call out oppression where they find it while learning to re-value women's ways of knowing and thinking.

By 2008, pedagogical theorists such as Heather E. Bruce, Shirley Brown, Nancy Mellin McCracken, and Mary Bell-Nolan were advocating pedagogical strategies designed to help teachers understand their own identities while simultaneously empowering students—regardless of gender binaries—in the high school English classroom. The classrooms they describe involve de-centered authority, rooms in which every student—female, male, transgendered, or questioning—has a voice, rooms in which emotions, ethics, and bodies are respected and empowered. Their emphasis implies much about the ways discourse can be used to empower students by destabilizing authority and making them aware of the relationships between language, community, identity, empowerment, and emotions—especially emotions.

Teacher Approaches and Discoveries

As previously noted, we conducted a study in which we provided four teachers with extensive questionnaires asking about gender and feminist practices in their classrooms. With what we knew about the scholarly literature we had examined in mind, our goal was to inquire about the teachers' self-identification as feminists and attendant practices in teaching literature. What emerged indicates that these teachers acknowledge the relationship between their understanding of feminism and the fallacy of thinking of gender in terms of binaries. All of these teachers write about the role of language and emotions in affecting cultural understandings of gender, and all of them think that asking students to identify gender issues in the books they read corresponds to the goal of teaching critical thinking skills. At least two teachers also talk about gender on a spectrum of empowerment that allows students who neither enact traditional gender roles nor identify with the oppressor or the oppressed in typical power dynamics to explore gender in multi-faceted ways.

Respondent A ("Amanda") teaches primarily freshmen in a mid-size charter high school; respondent B ("Bill") teaches all levels in a rural high school; respondent C ("Callie") teaches sophomores and A/P seniors in a large urban school; and respondent D ("Deidre") teaches juniors and seniors in a large suburban high school. We asked all teachers to comment on their feminist practices, on students' responses to feminism, and on texts they teach that communicate gender ideologies.

All respondents describe needing first to define feminism for students in ways that address both misconceptions and student hostility. As all note, many students continue to harbor binaristic stereotypes that cast feminists as (only) women who are (always) angry, rather than as people of both genders seeking equality and identity recognition.

Amanda's students begin the year "not really notic[ing] gender issues in the text." She gets "the occasional 'who cares?' from a male student early on when we talk about gender issues." Students tell her "everything is equal now between men and women." They "don't perceive that there are gender inequalities until we really unpack what they are and how gender roles in our society reinforce those inequalities." Bill and Callie have students who are more vocal in starting the year with negative connotations of feminism based more in their emotional registers than in intellectual or cognitive ones. Both report students who initially reject feminism as a "lesbian" value system. As Bill puts it: "I find that most students believe that a feminist outlook has a negative connotation attached to it." He finds that discussion is the best way to "set the record straight." Deidre, on the other hand, writes: "My students often come to me knowing that I am a feminist, yet few know exactly what this means."

Respondents discuss the importance of teaching students to be responsible for multiple analyses of their culture and the texts they read. Amanda describes wanting her students "to be aware of and responsible for a good portion of their learning." Deidre uses discussion and textual analysis to teach her students "to understand that the process of reading a text is political and social." For these teachers, reading texts is a way to learn to analyze culture, and discussion is a way for students to learn how to think and feel differently about feminism. For all four teachers, their self-consciousness about employing feminist pedagogies is an aspect of their teacher identity.

Amanda: Language, Social Constructs and Empowerment

Amanda recognizes that the pedagogy of critical thinking can lead to power imbalances. One of her concerns is the way that classroom debate leads to what she calls "intellectual bullying." To avoid such situations, Amanda asks freshmen to rely on Socratic dialogues wherein they prepare questions for each other and then prepare evidence to answer those questions. Students subsequently lead the classroom discussion. Moreover, Amanda uses YA novels, such as *The Hunger Games*, to provide students with examples of strong female protagonists operating under complex understandings of how gender identity can empower or disempower girls. By the end of the year, Amanda finds that freshmen who initially rejected concerns about sexism can discuss gender "in a safe, cooperative environment."

Amanda also notes that through her pedagogical choices students find multiple ways to experience gender and power, especially as they learn about social constructs:

The beauty of using social constructs as a lens is that gender discussions don't just revolve around the inequalities for women due to living in a patriarchal society. Especially after looking at the hero quest, typically carried out by males, it's an easy opening to discussing the limitations and absurdities of male gender roles in our society and literature. All students have experiences based on gender discrimination.

Ultimately, Amanda feels the best way to prevent students from thinking dualistically is to teach them about the relationship between language and social constructs. She writes: "Language is the most important tool we have to shape and change our worlds. We are empowered when we are able to define what is happening to us and what it is we do to those around us." For Amanda, her ability to teach critical thinking that considers larger issues of justice depends on asking students to think about gender as multivariate and socially constructed.

Bill: Female (and Male) Community

More than the other teachers in this study, Bill reports student resistance to discussions about gender—perhaps because he teaches in a rural area, or perhaps because he is male, which allows students to reject his identity as a feminist. Because these students do not perceive Bill in the role of the oppressed, they may not feel compelled to identify with his position. Bill writes about feminism:

> Most students seem to think that the issue is humorous in nature, and I attribute that to our poor cultural sensitivity and the media's portrayal of gender in general. Most students do not seem to realize that the "ignorant father" (a la *Everybody Loves Raymond*, etc.) is also an issue of gender. It can take a while for them to realize the issue is more pertinent and farther reaching than originally perceived.

Bill also finds himself providing a counter-balance to his students' tendency "to water down the issue to a very basic 'Who's better, guys or girls?' debate that I always have to reshape and mold into a more educated, informed approach." He reports that the most effective piece of literature in getting students to think about gender in non-binaristic ways is Laurie Halse Anderson's YA novel *Speak*.

> I teach this novel the first month of freshman year, and it features an abundance of power issues between teenage girls. This book really resonates with 99% of my students, as it opens up real dialogue about cliques and stereotypes they experience. The notion that teenage girls will turn on one another, and treat each other with such cruelty, is prevalent here, and students really respond with open minds and hearts. It can lead to some wonderful, insightful dialogue.

Bill is not afraid to confront the powerful emotions that *Speak* elicits through its intense portrayal of the aftermath of the rape of a fourteen-year-old girl by an older classmate. While he uses this novel to teach students to value female community over female competition, he also teaches that the issues presented are not just "of equality, but of attitude, focus, respect, integrity, and understanding that applies to both men and women." As students begin to grapple with the way power issues affect both genders, their thinking becomes more complicated: "Students seem to catch themselves in sexist language, and this is nice to see." Bill's ability to model feminism as a male authority figure provides him with a basic teacher identity that invites students across the gender spectrum to value community over competition and to see that both males and females have much to gain when gender stereotypes are dispelled.

Callie: Identity and Emotion

Callie believes students' initial inability to analyze gender is tied to their age and social class because most of them "have a mother that does, and has, stayed in the home to work, and thus the roles shown to them in their actual lives are often very traditional." She is also aware that her identity influences how students learn from her: "let's face it ... women *being* teachers is another traditional role ... . I might *be* a feminist ... but I am a woman in an *expected* role." Callie understands that her identity affects how her students position themselves in her classroom:

> In order to get conversations in which students really delve into their own opinions you need to create an atmosphere that creates comfort in doing so ... a space in which all opinions can be respected, part of this can only be done with teacher honesty and transparency ... which occasionally means saying something like "I think this is an area in which I am a little biased, I try to be fair, but I know I've a block up regarding X" ... not only does this allow your students real knowledge in how far they can go in some areas, but, as well, it forces a teacher to confront themselves ... something which I think is not done often enough. As teachers we often forget, or perhaps never learn, from where our own reactions to certain pieces of literature come; it is certainly worth investigation.

To help students overcome binary thinking of feminism "as something aggressive, angry, and potentially 'anti–Western society,'" Callie teaches a unit in the first semester in which she compares narratives from the same era, Kate Chopin's *The Awakening* and Joseph Conrad's *Heart of Darkness*, both written in 1899.

> Conrad's statements about the nature of women living in their own worlds "that would fall apart" if women were to ever have to deal with the reality of war, finance, pain, etc. is vastly different than what Chopin writes regarding

the same created social fantasy. Initially most students find Chopin MORE offensive than Conrad … this provides excellent areas of discussion.

Callie draws students' awareness to their anger and sense of injustice. Because they are still dependent on their parents, her students respond emotionally to Edna in *The Awakening* and criticize her for valuing her independence more than her children. By contrast, "the relationship to which Milkman relegates Hagar in *The Song of Solomon* taught in the second semester is taken on completely by the students themselves." By this time students begin to understand injustice in a more critical way—and to express their emotions about mistreatment based on broader gender issues rather than their own identity experiences.

Callie's willingness to examine her own identity in the classroom helps her students understand gender issues on a spectrum: "questions regarding gender issues become more natural as the year goes on." Like Amanda and Bill, Callie models feminist awareness as a teacher identity issue that enables her to teach gender in nuanced ways that allow students to admit to feeling injustice as an emotional and complex issue—even, they tell her, when examining texts outside of her classroom.

Deidre: Social Constructs and Self-Identity

Deidre is a self-conscious reformer, working actively to change the curriculum in her large suburban school district to ensure "that there is often a female protagonist that challenges androcentric norms" among the texts taught in the English classroom. Like Callie, she finds *The Awakening* to be a useful vehicle for teaching about gender in non-binaristic ways and "to consider the political and social constraints that held women to a higher moral standard than the male counterparts." Deidre—like Bill and Callie—reports the importance of studying historical context as a function of gender roles. Identity exploration is central to her students' understanding of gender: "High school students are quite interested in exploring gender differences. They are still working out their own sense of self and seemingly are quite anxious to openly discuss gender as a social construct."

Deidre teaches her students to notice how often they are asked "to identify with a male point-of-view" as one way of countering the type of binary thinking that makes women compete with each other. She does not teach YA novels because she believes that "many young adult novels have a female protagonist who is a victim of abuse." Although such novels as *The Disreputable History of Frankie Landau-Banks* and *The Hunger Games* openly address victimization and its attendant emotions, Deidre is still concerned that many YA novels are predicated on gender imbalance: "These protagonists overcome, but I worry that my students will see this victimization as a norm."

Deidre talks to her students about emotions as a key factor in self-aware gender identity, and she emphasizes the difficulty of thinking about gender without relying on binaries. Even while she questions basic assumptions about how gender has been constructed historically and how women are more often depicted in competition than community, she still acknowledges that women—and her female students— must exist within an educational environment that largely regards gender in terms of binaries.

These teachers all understand that their identities affect their students. They also believe that gender identity is fluid and not as easy to define as feminists might have indicated in their early work. Continually demonstrating that gender is a social construct provides an opportunity to deconstruct it in a way that critical thinking based on binaries does not allow. For these teachers, feminism allows students to question their thinking about sources of identity as they live within socially con-structed gender roles. Between them, they use literature to demonstrate issues of language, community, and emotional expression regardless of gender. Students come to see empowerment as it exists within a more complicated matrix of factors that leads to greater understandings of larger social justice issues.

One of our most interesting findings involves Amanda's and Callie's recognition that a lack of empathy creates a major obstacle to students' ability to think about gender, echoing Boler's conclusions about reluctant emotional response. In answer to the question "What are the chief obstacles to the feminist pedagogy of YAL in your classroom?" Amanda writes:

> Empathy. The chief obstacle to feminist pedagogy of YAL is getting students to be willing and able to see something from someone else's perspective, but that would be my answer for just about everything I teach. It is the most impor-tant expectation that I have and it is the most difficult concept for students to first understand and then embrace both developmentally and ideologically.

Callie writes that teaching feminism

> takes time, and it takes empathy … reminding boys that they are not "allowed" to cry when frustrated and hurt, and girls that when they do, the response is seen as weak and female … it takes going personal sometimes. When we relate literature to actual lived experiences the best conversations, and the best thinking, occurs.

Empathy undercuts binary thinking because it complicates an emotionally distanced, evaluative response with the messiness of emotional connection and sympathetic understanding.

Learning through Literature

While the teachers surveyed tend to teach books considered canonical, we find that much recent YAL that students pick up and read on their own helps scaffold critical thinking about language, community, identity, emotion, and empowerment, all issues both researchers and teachers we studied thought important. E. Lockhart's *The Disreputable History of Frankie Landau-Banks* is exemplary in this respect. Through a third-person narrative voice that is detached and focused, Frankie emerges as a careful critical thinker, a keen observer of hierarchy and group dynamics, and a strategist who weighs each word carefully to measure its potential effect before uttering it. During the summer between freshman and sophomore year, Frankie develops a body that earns her notice from Matthew, the most desirable boy at school. When Matthew chooses Frankie as his girlfriend, she gets the opportunity to observe how boys operate.

Frankie continually analyzes the way boys work to manage competitiveness and community through humor, and the way they smooth out potential conflict through self-effacement, turning even the most embarrassing situations into public performances of their superior position. Frankie also notes the degree to which the boys' public camaraderie is underwritten by their participation in a secret society called the Loyal Order of the Basset Hounds, an organization she knows about through her father, a former member. She spies on the Bassets and finds their activities banal, but realizes that the point of the group is not what it does but what it is: an exclusive, secret, boys-only club that requires loyalty for loyalty's sake. Frankie chafes at being excluded from the public and private community of boys and the fact that she is only welcome as Matthew's girlfriend and not on her own merits. She eventually realizes that "because of her sex, because of her age, because (perhaps) of her religion and her feminism, she could sit at their [lunch] table every day and she would never, never, ever get in" (195). She is angry that these boys rely on gender as a binary to justify disempowering and excluding females.

But Frankie is not one to accept the status quo. Throughout the text, readers learn that Frankie is a strategist. She recognizes when she is being manipulated, and she strategizes how she might use her already developed skills in debating, as well as her more nascent powers of sexual attractiveness, to get what she wants. The narrator alerts readers to Frankie's processes through anecdote and direct narration of her thoughts. Many of her reflections revolve around gender, but she is careful to parse gender as a social construct that carries with it confining expectations of behavior and attitude that she does not accept, even as she sees their utility. For instance, in the early stages of her relationship with Matthew, Frankie realizes that he likes her best when she behaves like someone who needs his help and accepts his opinions without serious challenge; because being his girlfriend grants her (albeit limited) access to his world, she plays her part. Eventually, Frankie rejects this position for herself, but not before she has thoroughly tested it. Significantly, she tests it most fiercely by asserting herself with her former boyfriend, Porter. When he tries to warn her about losing herself to Matthew, she yells at him for assuming she can't look out for herself. In the aftermath, she considers how she feels about her outburst:

> Frankie hadn't *liked* herself when she'd been yelling at Porter—but she'd admired herself. … She admired herself for taking charge of the situation, for deciding which way it went. She admired her own verbal abilities, her courage, her dominance.
>
> So I was a monster, she thought. At least I wasn't someone's little sister, someone's girlfriend, some sophomore, some girl—someone whose opinions didn't matter. (144)

The stakes with Porter are much lower than they would be had Frankie asserted herself with Matthew; after all, she still likes kissing Matthew, in addition to the power she enjoys from being his girlfriend. But she is clearly engaged in a project of thoughtful self-definition, of figuring out who she wants to be and whether it is more important to be loved or admired, a dilemma that persists until the end of the book. Gender is a large part of the mix, but mostly because for girls it is an impediment to power in a patriarchal society.

One of the most interesting metaphors for Frankie under this reading is her language play. Prompted by P.G. Wodehouse, she begins experimenting with what she calls "neglected positives"—words that exist only as parts of other words that make use of a negative prefix. For instance, Wodehouse's famous example is that "gruntled" should be the opposite of disgruntled, but, as Matthew is quick to instruct Frankie, this is not the case; they actually mean the same thing. But Frankie finds it amusing to play with these words, using "mayed" when she means the opposite of dismayed, and "turbed" as the opposite of disturbed, and so on. It is a quirky expression of a more serious structure; she realizes that Matthew sometimes makes her feel "delible," as in erased, as opposed to what she wants to be, which is indelible.

This linguistic play alerts readers to Frankie's more general take on the problematic of gender as a binary opposition. In a discussion with a classmate who is attempting to essentialize gender opposition through species comparison, she argues:

> Because once you say women are one way, and men are another, and say that's gotta be how it is in people, then even if it's somewhat true—even if it's quite a good amount true—you're setting yourself up to make all kinds of assumptions that actually really suck. (162)

Frankie understands gender as a construct, but also intuits she is disadvantaged by a system that posits girls as the neglected positives of boys. When she covertly takes over the Bassets, Matthew never once suspects her because he sees her as harmless, an extension of himself that does not legitimately exist without him, much like the neglected positives that Frankie invents. Moreover, his disregard of her language play shows her exactly what he thinks of those neglected positives: They are not in his dictionary, so they are wrong and impossible. They do not exist. Ultimately, Frankie embraces her anger and defines her limits: She will not succumb to her desire for Matthew because it means being someone who does not matter the way she wants to matter in the world; her critical thinking skills get a crucial assist from her emotions in figuring out the kind of woman she wants to become.

Katniss Everdeen of Collins' *The Hunger Games* is another emergent critical thinker grappling with numerous injustices contextualized by her gender. Set in a dystopic future, the novel details how the Capitol demands that each of the twelve districts in the U.S. send two adolescent "tributes"—a girl and a boy—to participate in the nation's Hunger Games each year. Only one "winner" can survive the games. Although the novel establishes a male–female binary, Katniss undercuts that binary, strategically analyzing how doing so can serve to her advantage. Before the games, she is her family's hunter and gatherer, so she uses her prowess with a bow and arrow to survive in the arena of the Hunger Games. Her partner during the games is Peeta Mellark, far more nurturing and emotionally perceptive than Katniss, although she shows her gentle side on several occasions. Katniss is highly analytical. She can assess who among the opponents relies on strength to win in combat and who relies on evasion and strategy. But Peeta has his own strengths. He is physically stronger and his emotional awareness enables him to earn the public's approval of Katniss and him as a team. In this novel, males and females display a broad range of traditional gender roles, but neither gender is the sole proprietor of any particular trait.

The players with the greatest advantage, however, remain those who know how to analyze what they observe. For example, Katniss changes the balance of the game when she observes that several of the stronger players have formed an alliance—but they are not protecting their food supply, which she finds "perplexing" (216) and "complex" (218). She tells herself: "There is a solution to this, I know there is"; consequently, she shrewdly figures out how to trip the landmines that these players have built to protect their stores (220). When the Capitol reverses an earlier decision to let two members of one team win, which pits Katniss against Peeta, she deduces how to call the rule-maker's bluff. Peeta tells her, "We both know they have to have a victor" (343–44), which inspires Katniss to realize that the best way to rebel against the institutional repressiveness of the games is to provide the Capitol with *no* winner. Evoking the double suicide in *Romeo and Juliet*, Katniss convinces Peeta that they should commit suicide simultaneously by eating toxic berries. The strategy works, and they are both proclaimed winners, although the President is clearly displeased that these two players have subverted the system. Katniss tries to offer the patriarchy an alternative to their binary thinking, but everyone is either a winner or a loser in the economy of the Hunger Games. The Capitol wants one winner—not two, and clearly they do not know, as Katniss has threatened, how to respond to the threat of no winner at all.

Throughout the novel, Katniss and Peeta value self-definition more than anything. Katniss's first success in pleasing the crowds watching the Hunger Games comes when she follows a mentor's advice to "be yourself" because people "admire your spirit" (121). She wins the game on her own terms—but still feels she is lying to Peeta and to Gale, the boy she hunted with before the games, because she cannot decide which of the two she loves. Katniss recognizes that emotions are not binaries and that empathy is messy. She rejects traditional gender roles, and she loves more than one person, exploding the binaries inherent in classic love triangles. Peeta, too, values self-definition, although he consistently knows he loves Katniss unconditionally. Before the games, he tells her: "I want to die as myself. … I don't want them to change me in there" (141). And Peeta does not change. He protects those about whom he cares, and he fights mercilessly against those corrupted by the system. Even in the final moments of the Hunger Games, he offers his life so Katniss can live—and when she dismantles the Hunger Game's binaries, he still knows who he is: "His smile is the same whether in mud or in the Capitol" (361).

The Hunger Game's most important feminist gesture may be its emphasis on empathy, which is presented in non-gendered ways. When they were children, Peeta empathized with Katniss enough to give her a loaf of bread from his family's bakery because she was starving, even though he knew he would be beaten for it. Bread thus becomes the novel's symbol of empathy in this nation named, appropriately enough, "Panem." Katniss identifies Peeta's loaf of bread as her first "hope," but she always acknowledges it came to her because of Peeta's empathy (32). Although Katniss cannot "even imagine" being beaten by her parents, she feels concern about the black eye his mother has given him because of the bread. When Katniss later discovers that Peeta's mother has no confidence in him, she can "see the pain in Peeta's eyes"—and reminds him that she has only been able to survive so long because he helped her when she was starving (90). Ultimately, Katniss thinks of Peeta as the "boy with the bread," and she does not want to lose him (297), although she struggles at the end of the novel, when she insensitively admits that she does not love him the way he loves her, which means that "the boy with the bread is slipping away" (374).

During the games, Katniss creates a female community with Rue, a tribute who reminds her of her sister. Katniss refuses to compete with this girl because she feels so much empathy for her. When Rue lies dying, Katniss cradles her, sings to her, and wreathes the girl's body in flowers to show the Capitol "that whatever they do or force us to do there is a part of every tribute they can't own" (237). Understanding the basic humanity of every individual is a prerequisite to feeling empathy—and to understanding the importance of social justice. Rue's district sends Katniss a loaf of bread to publicly thank her for her gentle treatment of Rue and to symbolically thank her for her empathy. For Katniss, strength and strategic thinking are a hollow victory without empathy because empathy allows her to think beyond binaries and disrupt the social constructs of both gender and injustice.

Between these two strong female protagonists, Katniss and Frankie, readers are exposed to characters who perceive the problem with being the neglected positives of boys and who employ critical thinking to reject binaries. They refuse to accept victim status and understand that community and self-acceptance play a role in social empowerment. While Frankie is empowered by manipulating language and Katniss through empathy, both characters display enough emotional complexity to be attracted to different males for differing reasons. Neither ends their story with the "happily ever after" denouement of many YA novels. Instead, Katniss and Frankie learn analysis can be an empowering tool—and weapon—best tempered by empathy.

Conclusion

Teaching critical thinking skills is a significant factor in any literature curriculum, but when critical thinking devolves into binaries, concepts of social justice become bankrupt and girls still suffer the continuation of age-old stereotypes. Education theorists such as Megan Boler are right in acknowledging that emotions complicate pedagogy; likewise, those like Janet Alsup are aware that teachers need to model the "difficult, messy, and complex" nature of identity for their students (5). When teachers like Amanda, Bill, Callie, and Deidre face student opposition to feminism in their classrooms, they are experiencing the binaristic thinking that implies one term in the binary (here "male" or "female") is better than the other. But when these teachers and others recognize the importance of language, community, identity, and empathy in teaching critical thinking skills, they acknowledge that the best way to explode binaries is to teach students to validate the emotional experiences of injustice.

Reading literature is one way to understand empathy, and YA novels such as *The Disreputable History of Frankie Landau-Banks* and *The Hunger Games* allow discussion about the intricate nature of empowerment and disempowerment—and empathy. Teaching YAL thus serves multiple purposes, including demonstrating how empowering girls involves deconstructing language, emphasizing community, and exploring identity. Because of the affective range of most YAL, the genre also lends itself to complicating what it means to be empowered, what it means to have an identity, and what it means to experience social justice—or injustice. If, as Amanda argues, a lack of empathy is the "chief obstacle to feminist pedagogy," then perhaps teaching novels that require *all* readers to experience a strong female's sense of injustice is one way to teach students to understand how complex issues of gender and empowerment really are.

Works Cited

Alsup, Janet. *Teacher Identity Discourses: Negotiating Personal and Professional Spaces*. Mahwah, NJ: Erlbaum, 2006. Print.

American Association of University Women's Education Foundation and Wellesley College Center for Research on Women. *How Schools Shortchange Girls*. Washington, DC: American Association of University Women's Education Foundation, 1992. Print.

Boler, Megan. "Taming the Labile Other: Disciplined Emotions in Popular and Academic Discourses." *Philosophy of Education* 1997. 416–25. Web.

Bowman, Cynthia Ann. "Gender Differences in Response to Literature." *Gender Issues in the Teaching of English*. Eds. Nancy Mellin McCracken and Bruce C. Appleby. Portsmouth, NH: Boynton, 1992. 80–92. Print.

Bracher, Mark. *Radical Pedagogy: Identity, Generativity, and Social Transformation*. New York: Macmillan, 2006. Print.

Bruce, Heather E., Shirley Brown, Nancy Mellin McCracken, and Mary Bell-Nolan. "Feminist Pedagogy Is for Everyone: Troubling Gender in Reading and Writing." *English Journal* 97.3 (2008): 82–89. Print.

Carlson, Margaret Anne Zeller. "Guidelines for a Gender-Balanced Curriculum in English." *English Journal* 78.6 (1989): 30–33. Print.

Cleary, Barbara A., and Mary C. Whittemore. "Gender Study Enriches Students' Lives." *English Journal* 88.3 (1999): 86–90. Print.

Collins, Suzanne. *The Hunger Games*. New York: Scholastic, 2008. Print.

Comley, Nancy R. "Father Knows Best: Reading around 'Indian Camp.'" *Gender Issues in the Teaching of English*. Eds. Nancy Mellin McCracken and Bruce C. Appleby. Portsmouth, NH: Boynton, 1992. 69–70. Print.

Croker, Denise L. "Putting It on the Table: A Mini-course on Gender Differences." *English Journal* 88.3 (1999): 65–70. Print.

Flynn, Gail. "Gender and Reading." *College English* 45.3 (1983): 236–53. Print.

Lockhart, E. *The Disreputable History of Frankie Landau-Banks*. New York: Hyperion, 2008. Print.

McClure, Lisa J. "Wimpy Boys and Macho Girls: Gender Equity at the Crossroads." *English Journal* 88.3 (1999): 78–82. Print.

McCracken, Nancy Mellin. "Re-gendering the Reading of Literature." *Gender Issues in the Teaching of English*. Eds. Nancy Mellin McCracken and Bruce C. Appleby. Portsmouth, NH: Boynton, 1992. 55–68. Print.

McCracken, Nancy Mellin, and Bruce C. Appleby, eds. *Gender Issues in the Teaching of English*. Portsmouth, NH: Boynton, 1992. Print.

A Nation at Risk. U.S. Department of Education. April 1983. http://www2.ed.gov/pubs/NatAtRisk/risk.html. Web.

O'Donnell-Allen, Cindy, and Peter Smagorinsky. "Revising Ophelia: Rethinking Questions of Gender and Power in School." *English Journal* 88.3 (1999): 35–42. Print.

Shor, Ira. "Using Freire's Ideas in the Classroom—How Do We Practice Liberatory Teaching?" *Freire for the Classroom: A Sourcebook for Liberatory Teaching*. Ed. Ira Shor. Portsmouth, NH: Boynton, 1987. 1–6. Print.

St. Pierre, Elizabeth A. "A Historical Perspective on Gender." *English Journal* 88.3 (1999): 29–34. Print.

LIST OF CONTRIBUTORS

Joanne Brown is a Drake University Professor Emerita of English. While at Drake, she taught fiction writing, adolescent literature, and American drama. She is the author of four books: *Presenting Kathryn Lasky* (Macmillan, 1998), *Declarations of Independence: Empowered Girls in Young Adult Literature* (Scarecrow, 2002), *The Distant Mirror: Reflections on Young Adult Historical Fiction* (Scarecrow, 2005), the latter two co-written with Nancy St. Clair, and *Immigration Narratives in Young Adult Literature: Crossing Borders* (Scarecrow, 2011).

Karen Coats is Professor of English at Illinois State University where she teaches children's and young adult literature. She is the author of *Looking Glasses and Neverlands: Lacan, Desire, and Subjectivity in Children's Literature* (University of Iowa, 2004) and co-editor, with Anna Jackson and Roderick McGillis, of *The Gothic in Children's Literature: Haunting the Borders* (Routledge, 2007). She also co-edited, with Shelby A. Wolf, Patricia Enciso, and Christine A. Jenkins, the *Handbook of Research on Children's and Young Adult Literature* (Routledge, 2010).

Jane Greer is Associate Professor of English and Women's and Gender Studies at the University of Missouri, Kansas City, where she teaches courses in composition as well as in the rhetorical performances and literacy practices of girls and women. She is the editor of *Girls and Literacy in America: Historical Perspectives to the Present* (ABC-Clio, 2003) and has published her research in a variety of journals, including *College English* and *College Composition and Communication*, as well as in edited collections. She is also the editor of *Young Scholars in Writing: Undergraduate Research in Writing and Rhetoric*.

Rosemary Horowitz is Professor of English and Co-Director of the Center for Judaic, Holocaust, and Peace Studies at Appalachian State University. Her research interests are in literacy studies, with a particular focus on writing in the Jewish community. In addition to publishing numerous articles and authoring *Literacy and Cultural Transmission in the Reading, Writing, and Rewriting of Jewish Memorial Books* (Austin & Winfield, 1997), she is the editor of the collections *Elie Wiesel and the Art of Storytelling* (McFarland, 2006) and *The Memorial Books of Eastern Europe Jewry* (McFarland, 2011). Forthcoming is another edited collection entitled *The Legacy of Yiddish Women Writers*.

Katie Kapurch is a Ph.D. candidate in Communication Studies at the University of Texas at Austin. She teaches English courses at Texas State University, San Marcos. Her research frequently considers the legacy of folkloric constructs, such as those of the vampire and the mermaid, in contemporary texts. Especially concerned with girls' media and culture, her dissertation explores how vampires in *Twilight* and other popular works speak to female adolescent experiences. Forthcoming in the edited collection *Genre, Reception, and Adaptation in the Twilight Series* is a chapter by Katie that examines the uses (and decline) of narrating voiceover in the *Twilight* films to interrogate the representation of girlhood in cinematic adaptations.

Dawn Latta Kirby is Professor of English and English Education and Associate Dean, College of Humanities and Social Science at Kennesaw State University. She taught high school for nine years and served as a high school English Department chair for four years. Dawn is the co-author of *Inside Out: Strategies for Teaching Writing* (Heinemann, 2004) and of *New Directions in Memoir: A Studio Workshop Approach* (Heinemann, 2007). She is currently working on a fourth edition of *Inside Out*, studying the impact of memoir on young adults' self-efficacy, and reading YAL avidly.

Mary Napoli is Associate Professor of Reading and Children's Literature at Penn State Harrisburg. She has published widely on multicultural literature, reader response, poetry, and girls' responses to popular culture texts, and has co-edited several books, including *African and African American Children's and Adolescent Literature in the Classroom* (Peter Lang, 2011) and *Teaching Literary Elements with Picture Books* (Scholastic, 2009). She is also author of *Selling the Perfect Girl* (Routledge, 2012). Mary serves on the Children's Literature Assembly Notable Children's Books Award committee, and the National Council of Teachers of English (NCTE) Award for Excellence in Poetry for Children committee.

Elaine J. O'Quinn is Professor of English and Women's Studies at Appalachian State University (ASU), where she co-directs the English Education Program and teaches courses in young adult literature and girls' studies. Recently, she spearheaded a Girls' Studies Minor at ASU and started a Special Collection on Girls Series Books for the ASU Belk Library. She has published numerous articles and has presented extensively. She has many book chapters in a number of collections, including

Teaching with Reverence (Palgrave, 2012), *Getting It in Writing* (Information Age, 2011), *Elie Wiesel and the Art of Storytelling* (McFarland, 2006), and *Teaching, Learning, and Loving* (Routledge, 2003). Elaine is a member of the Outstanding Teachers in Arts and Sciences at ASU, and has also received the Arts and Sciences Award for Outstanding Advisor, as well as the UNC Board of Governors Teaching Award.

Linda J. Rice is Associate Professor of English Education at Ohio University (OU) where she was awarded the James Bruning Teaching Fellowship for 2011–13. A National Board Certified Teacher, Linda taught middle and high school English for ten years. She is the author of numerous publications, including *What Was It Like? Teaching History and Culture through Young Adult Literature* (Teachers College Press, 2006) and *Exploring African Life and Literature: Novel Guides to Promote Socially Responsive Learning* (International Reading Association, 2007). Linda was awarded the distinction "University Professor" by the Center for Teaching Excellence at OU in 2006 and received the College of Arts and Sciences Outstanding Teaching Award in 2008.

Shayla Thiel-Stern is an Assistant Professor at the University of Minnesota School of Journalism and Mass Communication, where she specializes in critical media studies and the intersection of interactive and social media, culture, and identity specifically as related to youth and gender. She is the author of *Instant Identity: Adolescent Girls and the World of Instant Messaging* (Peter Lang, 2007) and has published chapters in *Girl Wide Web: Girls, the Internet, and the Negotiation of Identity* (Peter Lang, 2007) and *Mediated Girlhoods* (Peter Lang, 2011). She has also published scholarly articles in *Feminist Media Studies* and *Girlhood Studies: An Interdisciplinary Journal*.

Roberta Seelinger Trites is Professor of English at Illinois State University, where she teaches children's and young adult literature. She is the author of *Waking Sleeping Beauty: Feminist Voices in Children's Literature* (University of Iowa, 1997), *Disturbing the Universe: Power and Repression in Adolescent Literature* (University of Iowa, 2000), and *Twain, Alcott, and the Birth of the Adolescent Reform Novel* (University of Iowa, 2007), and co-edited, with Betsy Hearne, *A Narrative Compass: Stories That Shape Women's Lives* (University of Illinois, 2009). Trites has served as the president of the Children's Literature Association and editor of the *Children's Literature Association Quarterly*.

Beth Younger is Associate Professor of English and Director of Women's Studies at Drake University, where she teaches courses in Adolescent Literature, Women in Horror Film, and Feminist Theory. In addition to articles in *NWSA Journal* and *Rosebud*, she is the author of *Learning Curves: Body Image and Female Sexuality in Young Adult Literature* (Scarecrow, 2009). In 2007 she was awarded the Arts and Sciences Outstanding Teacher of the Year at Drake University. Her current projects include a literary biography of Maureen Daly, author of *Seventeenth Summer*.

INDEX